UNSPOKEN GAME

ANDREW BEAVER

For general information on our other products and services or for technical support, customersupport@unspokengame.com.

The author also publishes its books in a variety of electronic formats. Some content that appears in print may not be available in electronic books. For more information about UnSpoken Game products and services, visit our web site at www.unspokengame.com.

ISBN:
978-1-7343615-0-6 (Paperback)
978-1-7343615-1-3 (eBook)

Printed in the United States of America

Table of Contents

Introduction

Many self-help books will leave you with a sense of purpose; few will give you direction for acting on it. Likewise, those focused on "financial freedom" excel at defining the term, but typically lack any blueprints for achieving that very goal. In this book, I'll be sharing with you every step of my journey, both high and low, on the way to financial freedom.

I grew up in a single-parent household where my mother's priority was keeping the family's head above financial waters rather than teaching us how to excel financially. The most important lessons she passed down to us centered around doing whatever it took to "make it happen." My hard work ethic is a direct result of my mother's strength. She showed me there's nothing I can't do if I put my all into it and keep my eyes on the prize. The strategies you'll be reading about in this book might never have developed if not for the tenacity she instilled in me. Building on that foundation of self-discipline allowed me to study the ins and outs of finances, debt, and creating multiple streams of income, and to use them to my advantage.

My journey has been a successful one so far, but not without sacrifices along the way. I wish I could tell you I was able to kick back and enjoy the finer things in life from start to finish, but no reward comes without pain. I didn't waste time daydreaming about missed opportunities or having fun with friends regularly. I was all about saving money and eliminating debt. Time didn't matter as I threw myself into this intense learning process, ultimately reaping the rewards because I had set my sights on a singular goal. Failure just wasn't an option.

Over the course of my adult life, I believe I've found the key to financial freedom from scratch. It has nothing to do with family, friends, or someone handing you a $100,000 loan to kickstart your random venture.

It has everything to do with taking the time to budget, sacrifice some luxuries, save, network, set goals, and generate income in multiple ways. Each of these has been a vital phase of my journey. As you read this book and begin to gather helpful tips, it will be tempting to put it down and get started right away. Patience is a virtue, so time to hone in on it from this point forward. After riding along with me through the following chapters and learning from my mistakes, you'll emerge with a clear vision of the dos and don'ts of financial freedom. Not only will you realize that financial freedom is possible, but you'll also have a blueprint you can leverage to get there.

Just remember that this journey was uniquely my own and that adjustments will be necessary on your part to make it work for you. Nothing in life is free, except for the choices we make to live it to the fullest. However I can be of service, I'm grateful to be sharing this leg of it with you. Are you ready to make it happen?

Chapter 1: My Journey

To understand the impact of my journey to financial freedom, one must understand where it all began and why I sought it so intensely. Everything I encountered along the way, for me or against, has shaped me into who I am today. These obstacles made me stronger, smarter, and more aware than I would've been otherwise. Financial freedom was never about the money in and of itself, but about focusing on what truly adds value to my life. Having (or not having) money should never limit our ability to do what we're most passionate about. Too many of us spend our time chasing money rather than purpose. Financial freedom, then, isn't about making you rich; it's about evoking real and lasting change by putting an end to the rat race. I intend to make this possible for you through smart money management and purposeful tips.

Over the course of my life, I've had eight jobs and been fired from three of them. I was even fired from my first job, working at a local candy store during my freshman year of high school. I thought I was doing fine until I came into work one day, and the owner told me she was letting me go. I wasn't committed to the company, she said. Sure enough, I was on the brink of making the varsity track team and had no qualms about missing work for track meets. But while she may have been correct in her assumption, the mental defeat of losing my first job hit me hard. From then on through college, I prioritized academics and athletics.

My mother selflessly allowed me to do this, even as her friends were telling her I should get a job and help her pay the bills. Much to my benefit, she believed that receiving a quality education and experiencing the joys of youth were vital to optimal growth. Imagine my excitement when I was offered my second job as an external auditor for a regional accounting firm in my senior year of college. The outcome of this position turned out to be a repeat of the first, leaving me defeated and jobless. I should've known this role wasn't a good fit for me after my initial interview. Based on the comments I heard regarding hiring me over more qualified individuals, I suspected they were doing me a "favor" or meeting some quota. Whether or not I was correct in this assumption, I was happy to get a job right out of college. Throughout my tenure at that job, I struggled with feelings of inadequacy—what I later knew to be "imposter syndrome." The quality of my work—or lack thereof—didn't help my case, either. It took me longer than other auditors to complete assignments, and I struggled to adjust to being in an office for sometimes ten hours a day. The football field or the gym had always been my home away from home. I wasn't meant to sit still.

It was a tough pill to swallow: a desk job that came with bad posture and sore muscles was to be my daily life, Monday through Friday. Three months in, they let me go, stating it was due to my inability to perform at the level they were expecting. Once again, that feeling of not being good enough plunged me into a state of distress. What's more, I'd just started studying for the Certified Public Accountant (CPA) exam. Despite my inner doubts and diminished funds, I continued with the CPA exam and made it my 9 to 5—my 9 to 9. This schedule lasted for the first two (out of four) exams until I got into a comfortable routine.

I wasn't going to let one company's opinion change the trajectory of my career and success. Understanding that adversity comes to us all, I refused to lay down my hand just because life had dealt me an uncomfortable lesson. I set out to prove I could succeed, no matter the obstacle. Five months after being fired, I passed all four parts of the CPA exam on the first go and landed a job at a Big Four accounting firm. But the struggles continued. Still, I was pretty frugal and didn't take my first "young adult" vacation until the following summer. At that time, I felt like things were finally going in the right direction, and I could afford some relaxation time. I moved in with a relative, hoping to live rent-free and get my finances in order. Unfortunately, I ended up having to bail them out of their financial difficulties by paying two significant payday advance loans and covering their rent two months of rent. I decided to take the loss of moving into a one-bedroom apartment so that I could tackle my situation head-on, without distraction.

Back at the office, I was hardened enough to take constructive feedback, and network with individuals I knew had a successful track record. They helped me cut my teeth on a fledgling career. Armed by this experience, I pivoted into a consulting role that acted as a glorified staffing service. My first assignment was an internal audit for a mid-sized tech company. Because they were a new client, I had the added pressure of proving the quality of our services. After four months of working on that assignment, I hit a twelve-week dry spell of unassigned time that ended with me getting fired from yet another position. The reasoning for this termination? "Lack of dedication to the company vision." I'd seen coworkers get fired before me and knew it was only a matter of time before my turn came. Despite being prepared for that setback, I didn't fully understand the reasoning behind it. I might've appealed their decision, but what was the point? I packed my belongings and left—hurt, but not defeated.

I surprise myself when I think of how well I handled that third rejection. But perhaps I was already itching for a career change. Deep down, I knew that career positions weren't everlasting for me. I started looking into a range of ventures, quickly picking up the ins and outs of how I might capitalize on them. More importantly, I was beginning to realize that working my tail off to make someone else rich(er) wasn't my idea of a good time. I can't say for sure how *they* saw it, but my previous employers had picked up on something that took me a few years to realize: the moment I put one foot through their door, the other was already on its way out. Something had been calling me away from corporate life from the very beginning. Seeing that I valued my personal growth more than the growth of their company, they were prepared to replace me. In hindsight, they were doing me a favor by forcing me to see myself for who I really was. But I was ready to take a good long look in the mirror and pursue what really makes me…me.

Chapter 2: Creating and Achieving your Goals

While many of us have big dreams and aspirations, we don't always feel prepared to go after them. Too often, unexpected obligations and life seem to get in our way. Our jobs barely allow us to scrape by, especially when we have families to support, leaving us with little mental room to think about our futures when we're so focused on the present. Ultimately, what most of us lack isn't the motivation, but the *direction* and *guidance* needed to hit our goals. My lifetime goal of achieving financial freedom isn't just for my own satisfaction but in service of becoming a living example for future generations within my family and beyond. And so, before we even get into the financial side of things, I'm going to share with you four key strategies you can use to set and achieve your goals. Goal Setting will act as the foundation for the successes that are to come.

1. Decide What You Want

The first and most important step is to think about what you want in life and what will make you happiest. This part seems simple. *I want financial freedom! I want to build my own monopoly! I want to be a fitness model!* Those are some of my life goals, and I act on them daily. (Though my consistent donut runs might put a crimp in my fitness modeling career…but we won't discuss that here!) Whatever your goals might be, they must be your own. Copying someone else's will get you nowhere. What works for even the most successful businessperson in the world won't necessarily work for you. What you need is a purpose.

A goal without a purpose is more likely to fail when times get tough, and you start asking yourself, "What's the point of trying?" Take financial freedom, for example. What do you plan to do once you obtain it, and why do you even want it in the first place? Many would say they seek financial freedom so they can travel the world. That might sound amazing, but what happens once you've exhausted every continent and have seen all the things you dreamed of but still have four or five decades more of life to go?

Your goals should come with a bigger purpose. To determine that purpose, talk to friends and family. What have *they* noticed that brings you true happiness? And when are *they* happiest around *you*? Take their reflections seriously and use them to determine what you want in the long run. Don't rush this step. It sets the tone for all to follow.

Let's return to my quest for financial freedom as an example. I ask myself:

What does financial freedom mean to me?

This question is all about what I want most based on the options available to me. It's also a question best answered with more questions:

i. Do I *really* need $150,000 in savings while making money elsewhere?
ii. Do I *really* need to be making $80,000 a year in passive income with no formal job?
iii. Do I *really* want to work 40 hours a week to ensure my bills are paid and have leftover income to spend as I please?

None of these questions are more valid than the other, and any might be seen as the maximum fulfillment of financial freedom. Others would say they're not enough. Either way, it's up to us to figure out what financial freedom, and the larger goals it connects to, means to us.

Once I've got financial freedom, then what?

Have you ever accomplished something so important that you thought nothing could make you happier, only to find yourself unsatisfied and yearning for the next challenge a few months later? Whatever your goals might be, the first thing to determine is whether they're just something cool you'd like to cross off your bucket list or whether they're sustainable and will grow into something truly meaningful over time. As children, we often ask, "Why?" even when we're given an answer, but as adults, we lose that curiosity. So whenever people come to me with questions about their own quest for financial freedom, I always make sure to ask them, "What next?" I often hear the same motivations with regard to pursuing financial freedom: the freedom to travel, buying a fancy house, and/or quitting one's job. While these are certainly amazing goals to have, and people should strive for them if that's their desire, at some point our excitement fades as we get used to things and we're left thinking, "What am I doing with my life?" Without taking the time to understand the "Why" behind the "What," we'll always be one step behind the joy and peace so fundamental to a fulfilled life.

2. Track Those Wants

Now that you've determined what you want, it's time to write it down in detail. I like to use the top-down approach by refining my long-term goals into smaller, more actionable chunks based on the following tiers:

***Long-term*:** Included in this tier are goals requiring three or more years for achievement. These are larger in nature and consist of multiple stepping stones. Such goals might include losing a hundred pounds, paying off your student loans, or starting a new business. In general, your long-term goal should exceed even your own expectations. That way, you're always motivated to push forward, setting the bar higher and higher for yourself along the way.

***Short-term (Annual)*:** Short-term or annual goals are a subset of the long-term goal and should be completed, as the name implies, within a year's timeframe. Annual goals are more detailed than their long-term counterparts, serving as the frame of those big-picture goals. If one of my long-term goals, for example, is to have a monopoly on the sports development industry, then my short-term goal for this year might be to establish a sports training platform that gains significant popularity locally, then across the US.

***Quarterly*:** Quarterly goals must be completed in a three-month span and should have a four-quarter build-up toward hitting an annual goal. Continuing with the above example, in this phase, I might ask myself, "What must I do over the next three months to get my first sports training platform (The Drill Factory) up and running?" My goal for the first quarter is to build a prototype of The Drill Factory and obtain enough feedback to make the appropriate adjustments prior to a full launch next quarter. This goal hits that sweet spot of being too big to get done in a day but realistic enough to complete within the quarter.

***Monthly*:** When it comes to monthly goals, I get even more specific about what needs to be actioned within the month to achieve my quarterly goal(s). In this case, the first month is dedicated to building a prototype, the second to conducting weekly focus groups, and the third to finalizing my prototype and finding the right developer for the job. Thus, what at first seems like an overwhelmingly difficult goal becomes doable when broken down into more manageable parts.

***Weekly*:** Finally, I always ask myself what I'm going to accomplish on a weekly basis. At this stage, I like to add "non-mission" goals—such as getting to bed by 11 p.m. and waking up at 5 a.m.—that help me be more efficient or stay mentally afloat. Such goals are important to include because success is a holistic enterprise: it depends on a balance of every aspect of life. Once these goals are properly included, I focus on quantitative goals to keep myself accountable. Considering the second month of the quarter, I might set a weekly goal to hold ten focus groups, spend ten hours a day drafting the wireframe for the prototype, and another hour daily taking time to understand my competitors. All of this helps me be more efficient with my time while ensuring that key areas of the mission are progressing.

Now that I have these goals firmly in mind, I track them using an "Action Tracker" spreadsheet (a template of which is provided in the Resources section). The Action Tracker keeps my goals fresh and serves as a "job well done" reminder when I need that extra energy boost. Sometimes a glance at the strides I've made so far is enough to revive my motivation when the going gets tough.

3. Let People Know

So, here I am with a bunch of solid ideas. I've written them down, along with actionable tasks. The blueprint is in my hands. What's next for me? The first thing I do is to force myself to say it loud and say it proud, "I'M WORKING TOWARD MY GOALS!" Some people, especially those who prefer to act rather than speak, shy away from this. But it's important to start letting people know about your journey and how excited you are to be on it. Too often, we fear judgment or having our ideas stolen, but it's rare that anyone who does so will have the means to capitalize on what they've stolen. Speaking freely about your journey has the following benefits:

1. *It brings your goals to the surface*: By giving voice to your ideas, you're imbuing them with life instead of leaving them to the fantasy of what could be. Other people's curiosity will constantly remind you of the goal in question, keeping you accountable at every step of the way. The more you work on your plan, the more you'll want to talk about your progress, and vice versa.

2. *Positive (and negative) feedback opportunities*: Positive reinforcement builds confidence and motivation. It's a bright light in an otherwise dark journey that not many are willing to endure. Then there's negative (or development) feedback, which, though hard to hear, often tells us when we need to pivot away from something that isn't working. One thing you must *never* do is let those criticisms shut you down completely. The reason for this is simple: Only those who care about your idea will be honest enough to tell you what's wrong with it. In other words, if no one was interested in or compelled by your idea in the first place, they'd just ignore it. But sometimes the ones who pick apart your ideas are giving you the best advice. Take that criticism with gladness of heart and use it to your advantage.

3. *Potential for partnership and mentorship*: Just as there are those who might try to bring you down, there are others who will be there to lift you up. These are the ones whose skills might best serve you in the context of a partnership or mentorship. I've spoken, for example, to established individuals who make up for their lack of background in sports training with their vast knowledge of business development. With their help, I've been able to think more deeply about the risks of operating a sports training business. If you feel strongly about keeping your idea private, don't hesitate to draw up a non-disclosure agreement. Be prepared, however, for tarnished trust and diminished interest from other valuable resources.

4. Take Action *Now*

Having dreamed all you can dream, planned out more than enough details to get started, and spread the word about our journey, you're now ready to take action. The keyword here is "action." From this point forward, you'll be in constant motion until you've reached your goals. But rest assured that what makes this part so frustrating is also what makes it so rewarding. You will fall short of certain goals, or even lose enthusiasm. But you *must* keep actioning your goals, regardless of what comes. The more you can minimize the distractions of failures, naysayers, and setbacks, the more you'll grow. This is why keeping track of every step is so important. By looking back at the goals you've laid out and the achievements you've already made on the way to getting there, you remind yourself that this is really happening, that you can do this. By reading this chapter alone, you're already taking the first step toward a goal you might not have even defined yet. The path is now open to you. What are you waiting for?

Chapter 3: Debt Elimination

Eliminating all of my debt was no easy task. In college, I fell victim to three common misunderstandings:

1. *Refund checks are free money*: A refund check is *not* free money and *does* accrue interest. I happily used my refund checks to pay for rent, video games, and other miscellaneous items over the course of my college career. Had I been more strategic, I would've left it alone or invested before spending it on things I wanted but didn't need.

2. *Consolidating student loans works for everybody*: I consolidated $40,000 in debt, thinking this is what everyone does to lower their payments. Had I fully understood debt consolidation, I would have tackled my small loans instead by using the avalanche strategy I discuss later in this chapter.

3. *Six-month student loan deferment means no accruing of interest*: No student loan payments for six months? Yeah, I'm going to take advantage of this system to the very end! The joke was clearly on me. Sure, my credit wasn't negatively affected by non-payment, but it wasn't as if the loan companies were handing out free money. In fact, I was so naïve; I didn't realize interest had been accruing throughout my five years of school.

I didn't realize how deep a hole I was digging for myself by deferring my loans until I started looking at my payments in detail. Since I was only skating by on the minimum allowed payments, I wasn't even cutting into the principal amount. This had gone on from graduation in 2011 to 2015, at which point I told myself that enough was enough. For context, I had $40,000 in student loans, a $17,000 car note, and approximately $5,000 in consumer debt built up before my elimination journey started. In a year and a half, I was completely debt-free.

Here's how I did it.

First, I had to understand the various kinds of debt out there and how they impacted my finances. Loans generally fall into two categories: installment loans and personal loans. Installment loans are paid over a period of time with a set number of scheduled payments. Examples include mortgages, car notes, and student loans. Personal loans, also known as consumer loans, are your typical credit card loans (and all the bad decisions that go with them). My credit card woes started during my senior year of college when my roommate lost his job and decided to break our lease only two months in. Despite my best efforts to be understanding and work things out with him, it never panned out. With no job to cover this sudden and unexpected rent increase, I resorted to credit cards and the occasional dip into the "Mommy I need help!" emergency fund. I took jobs from staffing companies on weekends to make some extra cash, but it was never enough. All the while, I was bearing that interest hit until I got aggressive with payments in 2015. Since then, I've learned to use credit cards to my advantage rather than as a bailout measure. Below are common examples of debt, followed by some practical ways to get rid of it.

Mortgages: A mortgage is a loan you take to purchase a home. Your bank or loan originator sets the terms of the loan, including the down payment amount, interest rate, and/or premium mortgage insurance (PMI). When purchasing a home, it's crucial to get the right financing, or you'll be setting yourself up for a long and difficult road ahead. I would consider the following loan types when looking to add a property to your assets.

Conventional: A conventional mortgage is provided through a bank. That bank will ask for anything between 10-20% as a down payment. If you put in anything less than 20%, some banks may require you to pay PMI. This option requires sufficient documentation regarding your credit standing, salary details, and capital, and gives you the greatest flexibility regarding the type of property you may purchase.

Federal Housing Authority (FHA) insured loans: FHA is a program designed for first-time homebuyers or individuals who don't have an existing FHA mortgage. It requires a 3.5% down payment—$7,000 down, for example, on a $200,000 home—and the interest rate is consistent with that of a conventional loan. This option comes with stricter loan requirements and restrictions on the types of houses you may purchase; whatever home you choose must meet a number of standards during the appraisal process for it to qualify.

Other: Depending on your location, there may be additional first-time homebuyer programs available to walk you through the process. These programs likely also allow for low down payments, low-interest rates, and may sometimes waive PMI. I recommend being diligent in your research to ensure this is right for you. Such programs are generally quite stringent—sometimes requiring that properties be move-in ready, for example. Consider all factors before committing to any mortgage agreement.

Car Notes: A car note is a loan you take to purchase a car. Interest rates for car notes can skyrocket beyond those of mortgages, which must submit to some form of government regulation to keep them relatively stable. Fail to pay attention to car financing terms, and you may be hit with high-interest rates (8-25%) comparable to credit card loans. In that case, you'd do well to think about other car financing strategies such as leasing, or even consider driving services and/or public transportation. A clean credit report, a history of on-time payment for installment loans, a stable salary, and a sizable down payment are all good ways to lower your interest rate.

Student Loans: There are many types of student loans, but for our purposes, let's focus on federal and private loans.

Federal loans: Federal loans generally have low and fixed interest rates when compared to private loans. Depending on the industry you enter after leaving school, there may be loan forgiveness programs or flexible payment plans available to alleviate the stress of paying off your loans. The company to which you pay your loans is chosen by the federal government or school, so their repayment options will differ. Spend some time researching the various federal loan programs and determine if any of them make sense for you.

Private loans: Private loans provide more flexibility based on an individual's financial status. If a fixed rate is not preferred, variable rates or a combination of both may be offered. Private loans are similar to mortgages, and car notes in that credit history, salary, and other factors can affect your interest rate.

Personal/Consumer Loans: These include your lines of credit and credit card balances. Unless you've become very seasoned in your financial responsibility, I strongly encourage you to steer clear of credit card debt altogether. Though I discuss in a later chapter how I capitalized on my long-term efforts to develop strong credit, even I am wary of allowing my outstanding credit card balances to grow out of control.

Now, let's move on to the steps for eliminating debt.

1. *Layout all your debt in a spreadsheet or document.* This includes all the debt types listed above. Make sure to include the interest rate, balance, payment date, due date, and the monthly payment (broken down by interest and principal payments) for each item. Once you have your debt laid out, the next step is to create a payment schedule for each debt balance to determine how long it will take to pay off. This will give you a full picture of your debt position and allow you to see whether any additional steps are needed.

2. *Lower your interest rate.* After you've itemized your debt to the point where the mere sight of it burns a hole into your very soul, it's time to determine your best approach to lower interest rates across the board. A

range of refinancing strategies can help you do this. Consider the following four options:

a) *Peer-to-peer lending*: Peer-to-peer lending allows investors to crowdfund loans and generate passive income. Such investors can get you an unsecured loan on your high-interest balance at a lower rate. You will have to provide personal information such as salary, credit score, profession, and other information, similar to the asks of any loan originator. When utilizing this strategy for credit cards or home improvements, you'll be expected to refinance based on a certain number of years (e.g., a three- or five-year note). This will create accountability for making payments, as the full balance will be due within the next three or five years.

b) *Debt consolidation companies*: Debt consolidation companies are like peer-to-peer lenders, except that they typically require some form of collateral. They will either consolidate or simply refinance a balance to give you a lower interest rate. The said rate is determined by multiple factors, including the length of the new loan. When I approached debt consolidation, I personally took the lowest loan rate with the goal of paying off the entire balance within a year, no matter what. Working with a debt consolidation agency requires making payments greater than the minimum balance.

c) *Balance transfers*: Balance transfers involve moving a debt obligation from one entity to another in an attempt to achieve more favorable terms. This strategy is optimal for consumer debt. Many credit card companies provide low- or no-fee balance transfers to obtain a lower interest rate. Not only do they provide lower interest rates; they may also provide an interest-free period of up to 18 months, giving you leeway to strategize and make smaller balance payments while focusing on your high-interest credit cards.

For example, say you have two credit cards, A and B, with $1,000 (16.99% interest) and $2,000 (14.99% interest) in debt, respectively. You get approved for a third credit card, C, for a $1,000 line of credit at 17.99%

interest, along with the option of doing a balance transfer at 0% for an introductory period of 18 months. In order to take advantage of the balance transfer, you must pay a balance transfer fee of $5 or 5% of the total balance, whichever is greater. The chart below illustrates your interest savings depending on whether you transfer the full balance from credit card A, transfer a portion of credit card B's balance or do not take advantage of the balance transfer at all.

Example of Balance Transfer Benefits

	Credit Card A	Credit Card B	Credit Card C	Balance Transfer Fee	Annual Interest/Fee	Annual Savings
	17%	15%	0%	5%		
No Balance Transfer	$ 1,000	$ 2,000	$ -	$ -	$ 470	$ -
Pay off A	$ -	$ 2,000	$ 1,000	$ 50	$ 350	$ 120
Apply to B	$ 1,000	$ 1,000	$ 1,000	$ 50	$ 370	$ 100

In this scenario, you'll save approximately $100 to $120 in interest annually by taking advantage of balance transfers for either credit card. The larger the balance, the greater the savings potential. The obvious caveat to the balance transfer strategy is that you must expect to pay it off by the end of the introductory period. As you can see, credit card C has a higher interest rate than cards A or B once the introductory period is over.

d) *Calling a credit card company*: One potential way to lower the interest rate on a credit card is to simply call your credit card company and see if they can lower your interest rate or give you an interest-free promotional period. This isn't guaranteed to work, but you may just get lucky. I periodically call my credit card companies and request an interest-free period or rate adjustment on my cards. Most companies would prefer to lower your rate than lose you as a customer if you make them aware that you're considering a balance transfer.

e) *401k loan provision:* Taking out a loan against your 401k could prove to be very beneficial if you're able to do so. This method differs from an early withdrawal, which involves withdrawing your 401k prior to turning 59½ years old. If you decide to withdraw funds from your 401k early, you may be hit with a 10% additional tax penalty, and the gross withdrawal will be included in your taxes at your applicable tax rate. Note that there are instances when an early withdrawal may not result in a penalty—for example, when paying a medical insurance premium subsequent to job loss. The 401k loan provision allows you to borrow from your own 401k for a set number of years at a specified interest rate. Should you end up leaving your company prior to paying back the loan in full, you'll be required to do so or subject that balance to the early withdrawal penalty. Restrictions on the loan amount vary between companies. I, therefore, suggest reaching out to your Human Resources department to fully understand the restrictions that apply to you.

3. *Determine your long-term strategy*: Once you've minimized your interest rates, it's time to figure out which balance to attack first. The Avalanche and Snowball methods are two ways that, if applied correctly and consistently, can help you achieve debt elimination in a timely manner.

Avalanche method: With this method, you make minimum payments on all of your balances except for the one with the highest interest rate. For example, if you've allocated $1,000 to pay down five of your debt balances, all the additional money past the minimum is placed on that highest card.

Example of an Avalanche Debt Payoff

	Payoff Order	Balance	Interest Rate	Min. Monthly Payment	Monthly Interest	Annual Interest
Credit Card D	1	$ 4,000	17%	$ 835	$ 57	$ 680
Credit Card C	2	$ 3,000	14%	$ 25	$ 35	$ 420
Credit Card A	3	$ 1,000	12%	$ 50	$ 10	$ 120
Credit Card B	4	$ 2,000	11%	$ 30	$ 18	$ 220
Credit Card E	5	$ 5,000	10%	$ 60	$ 42	$ 500

After paying off the balance with the highest interest rate, you keep moving on to the next highest rate down the list until all of your debt is paid off. Doing this will minimize the amount of interest you end up paying. In the above example, credit card D will charge you more in the long run, as evident in the annual accrued interest. The disadvantage of this strategy is more psychological than anything. If you have a large balance comprised of many loans, it may take you much longer to pay off that debt. Chipping away at such a slow rate may hurt your motivation, but reminding yourself of the final result will help you look forward. If you're the type who insists on seeing debt go away quickly, then the next strategy may suit you best.

Snowball method: This method flips the terms of the previous one by making minimum payments on all of your balances except for the one with the *lowest* balance. Unlike the Avalanche method, here you focus on eliminating your overall *number* of loans, leaving you able to focus on your largest balance.

Example of a Snowball Payoff

	Payoff Order	Balance	Interest Rate	Min. Monthly Payment	Monthly Interest	Annual Interest
Credit Card A	1	$ 1,000	12%	$ 835	$ 10	$ 120
Credit Card B	2	$ 2,000	11%	$ 20	$ 18	$ 220
Credit Card C	3	$ 3,000	14%	$ 40	$ 35	$ 420
Credit Card D	4	$ 4,000	17%	$ 60	$ 57	$ 680
Credit Card E	5	$ 5,000	10%	$ 45	$ 42	$ 500

This method allows for small wins until you have the confidence and consistency to take on the bigger and more challenging balances. The disadvantage of this strategy is that you will be paying more interest in the long run, and so your debt will stay with you longer. Between these two methods, I prefer Avalanche because I'm big on not overpaying for anything. If I can minimize the number of additional fees I'm charged in any situation, I will. Check out the Resources section for "Debt Paydown" templates that you can use to begin plotting your path to a debt-free life.

The final step of debt elimination is to make yourself accountable by implementing these new payoff schedules into your budget and sticking to them. The perfect spreadsheets and templates mean nothing without action and commitment. You can do this.

Chapter 4: The Seven-day Budget

You only need seven days to perfect your budget. Anything beyond that, and it'll never happen. Do you ever wonder where your money is going day after day, month after month? Creating a budget may seem a bit daunting, but in this Chapter, I lay out a seven-day plan that, if followed, will set you up for the financial freedom you desire.

Days 1-3: Understanding where you stand financially

There are three major steps to understanding where you stand financially: knowing your credit standing, expenses, and income.

Credit Standing

Your credit standing starts with your credit report. A credit report gives you a full and (sometimes painfully) honest picture of your financial situation. The Fair Credit Reporting Act (FCRA) requires each of the major national credit reporting companies—Equifax, Experian, and TransUnion—to provide a free copy of your credit report at your request once every 12 months. Treat these free reports as an opportunity to hone in on your situation without compromise. A credit score is easily obtained through your credit company, assuming they provide the service. These companies provide monthly updates on your credit score and status of your creditworthiness. Your credit score gives you a bookmark for where you currently stand. The score itself doesn't necessarily matter as you focus on the budgeting process, and in any case, once you're financially free with a clean credit report, you'll no longer desire that "hallowed" 800+ credit score.

A high credit score indicates nothing more than the fact that you're great at paying people back. A great quality to have, to be sure, but even when

I eliminated all of my debt, my credit score dropped slightly. I was clearly financially responsible, so why should I be required to owe somebody something to maintain a high score? Keep in mind that once you get to 750, it's unlikely you'll receive any additional benefits from going higher. When you apply for credit, you'll receive the same low-interest rate and payment desired at 800 as you would for 750. Anything beyond that is nothing more than vanity.

It's best to use your credit report as a diagnostic tool to determine which, if any, accounts are delinquent, and how you can go about having these accounts removed from your report. In some cases, collection companies will settle on a payoff amount or provide a discounted monthly payoff plan. Identifying your delinquent accounts is the only way to understand how they fit into the overall picture of your expenses.

In order to understand how and where you spend your money, you must look at your recurring and consistent monthly expenses. Start by looking at your last three bank statements, listing the most frequent expenses, and totaling them up. This allows you to put a concrete dollar amount on your monthly spending. When listing expenses, always take a conservative approach. In other words, if the money you spend on eating out ranges between $60 and $120 per month, then conservatively estimate that expense at $120 per month. The following is a list of typical expenses (be sure to include due dates, where applicable). I will return to these later in the chapter:

Home
- Rent/mortgage
- Electricity
- Renters insurance
- Heat
- Water
- Laundry
- Groceries

Car expenses
- Gas
- Car insurance
- Car note (interest rate, total balance, monthly payment)
- Maintenance
- Tolls
- Commuter rail
- Uber/Lyft

Student loans (interest rate, total balance, monthly payment)
Credit cards (interest rate, total balance, monthly payment)
- Credit card 1
- Credit card 2
- Credit card 3

Nightlife/entertainment
- Restaurants (monthly – use Mint)
- Alcohol
- Entertainment
- Netflix
- Hulu
- Amazon Prime
- Cable
- Spotify
- Premium Channels (HBO, Showtime, etc.)

Other expenses
- Phone (cell and/or landline)
- Gym membership
- Medical bills
- Child expenses
- Family expenses (e.g., the "Can I borrow 100 dollars until next year?" loan)

The next step is relatively straightforward and involves writing out your consistent monthly income. For salaried employees, only account for what you receive each month. If your paychecks are inconsistent, be conservative by calculating your estimated amount based on the lowest pay you'll receive monthly or by averaging the last three months' worth of paystubs. You should also take into account any hustles you've got on the side.

You'll then need to figure out your net income (loss) before making any adjustments. This will help you determine whether any significant lifestyle changes are in order. This is the most time-consuming and detail-oriented part of the process, but it's worth it. It's the foundation for all that follows, so make it strong.

Days 4-5: Adding and reducing

Here we'll be focusing on keeping that net income (loss) figure out of the red. This requires you to determine what's preventing you from saving money every month, and it begins by answering the following three questions.

What significant expenses do I have?

I could dedicate this entire book to reducing or eliminating expenses, but the following are some ways I found particularly helpful.

Review your monthly subscriptions: Monthly subscriptions are a great way for businesses to make money. They're also a great way for consumers to lose money consistently. Almost always, we buy into subscriptions with genuine excitement, only to find that we take advantage of their services far less often than we planned. How do we counter this? To start, gather a small group of people who share your financial goals and start determining which memberships you might join together. Many membership services offer family or group plan options that could save you money. As of this writing, cell phone plans drop from $80 a month per person in a solo plan to $40 per person in a family plan for the exact same services. You can also get rid of the subscriptions altogether, saving you even more, so keep only those you deem necessary.
Move: Are you sacrificing more than 50% of your monthly income for rent just because you're living alone? According to financial experts, your rent should never exceed 30% of gross income. If you *are* surpassing 30%, you have a few options. One is to get a roommate or two to split not only rental costs, but also utilities, cable, and other expenses. Another is to move back in with your parents or family. Are you worried about the stigma against living with family as a young adult? Don't be. Pride should be furthest from your mind when you're on the road to financial freedom. Parents will more than likely allow you to live significantly below market

value for rent if they understand your goals and how dedicated you are to attaining them. Just be prepared to make your bed every morning per parental orders. If, for whatever reason, the idea of living with your parents is too much to handle, consider moving away from urban centers. But be aware of the tradeoffs. What you gain in cheaper rent, you lose in the long commute. This can be an expense in and of itself, both financial and emotional, and so the distance may only be worth it if the savings are exceptional.

Curb or sell that car: Cars are extremely expensive. Public transportation, unappealing as it may be, is nevertheless a viable alternative. Tally up how much you spend on your car alone and ask yourself: Is the extra cost really worth it?

The "Is it really worth it?" question is, of course, one you should be asking yourself of *every* expense. Other questions you should consider asking yourself:

- Can I carpool instead of drive?
- Cook at home instead of restaurants?
- Set a weekly eating out budget?
- Set a weekly entertainment budget?
- Do I really need to go out *every* week?
- Should I consolidate debt or refinance?

Where am I spending my time?

Something people often forget to consider when assessing their monthly net income (loss) is where they spend their time outside of work. Whether your time is spent watching TV, surfing social media/internet, eating out, or hanging out with friends (e.g., bowling, drinking, partying), you must be honest and assess the cost benefits of your leisure time. This starts with listing every activity and thinking about how much time is being devoted to each. Regardless of how well you think you know yourself, it's best to keep an accurate log for the next two weeks to gain an accurate picture of your time. Once you have your weekly time laid out, you should divide the list between productive and non-productive categories. Your goal will be to reduce your non-productive time and increase your productive time with your monthly spending and savings in mind. Additional questions to ask yourself when looking to eliminate wasted time include, "Do I have a lot of idle time when I could be working on myself?" and "Am I doing anything that doesn't make me happy or better?"

How can I generate additional income?

Once you understand how and where your time is being spent, you can work on eliminating wasted time and filling that space with additional revenue streams, which might include anything from working overtime, taking on a second job, or getting your side hustle on. Below are some of my favorite cost-effective side hustles.

Rideshare services: Whether by driving your own car or renting it out to others, rideshare companies allow you to generate additional money on your own terms. These companies provide flexible hours and a profit potential that's limited only by your willingness to put in the hours. A friend of mine, for example, made over $11,000 per month for three months in a row by offering rides through such a service. He achieved this by working 12-hour days, seven days a week, in the San Francisco Bay Area. It might seem like a grueling schedule, but it goes to show that the money *is* there if you can put in the effort. There are, of course, extra costs associated with this line of work, including increased wear and tear on your vehicle, along with increased insurance premiums due to your car being used as a commercial vehicle. Your efforts must, therefore, be enough to make it worthwhile by transcending those expenses into profit.

Yard sale/Goodwill flipping: This venture isn't for the faint of heart. The objective of yard sale/Goodwill flipping is to find hidden gems at significant discounts and resell them online for their true market value. During a four-month span of casually finding discounted items to sell, I sold 136 products for a gross profit of approximately $3,800. The total cost for those items was around $2,000, netting me $1,800 in profit. Being the conservative person that I am, I vowed to resell each product within a reasonable timeframe (seven days or less from the time of purchase). Had

I been willing to wait longer, my net profit would've been significantly higher. This venture requires market research. Before you buy a single item, look carefully at online merchants that allow for used product sales to figure out which products are selling well and quickly. Once you've found a handful of products you'd like to target, scope them out at yard sales. If the prices are too high and the seller won't allow you to bargain, move on. The real money is made through your research, not just at the time of purchase and ultimate delivery.

Small-service companies: Do you have the time flexibility to take on odd jobs? Opportunities exist for you to name your task and generate a profit. That task could be as small as proofreading someone's homework to landscaping their entire property. If you can do it, there's an opportunity to make money from it. I've often used such services for presentations, graphic design work, and work/home cleanings, among others, and I've found that many do an admirable job.

Sell your skillset: If you believe your skill or ability is professional enough, consider going into business for yourself. If you have a job, then you're developing a skill. Think about what that skill is and how you can capitalize on it. As an internal auditor, I looked at financial statements constantly with an eye toward figuring out how to improve their internal processes for the most important line items. Sometimes I forgot that through this process, I was learning a significant amount about how businesses operate, how they think, and ways to make them more profitable. It seemed a shame not to apply those 6+ years of experience I'd gained to small business consulting. As I detail in a later chapter, I did exactly that, but through lessons learned on the football field instead of the accounting office.

An online search for top ways to make additional/passive income is an ideal place to start. Here are some examples of skill sets currently in high demand:

Fitness Coach
Private Chefs
Mobile Application Development
Social Media Marketing
Translation
People Management
Blogging/Vlogging
Website Design and Development

Decide what works for you and your schedule—and by that, I mean your *actual* schedule, not your Netflix binging schedule. Pick a venture that provides not only additional income but also a sense of purpose in the service of your goals.

Days 6-7: Set up savings/investment accounts

If you've gotten this far, then consider yourself prepared to move forward. These last two days are going to set you apart from the rest of the pack. The following are five accounts I suggest setting up to start. As your money management skills improve, these accounts can be nuanced at an even greater level of detail.

Bills checking account: This account is used for monthly and consistent bills. When you're able to automatically allocate your bill money each month without touching the extra, you can confidently know that your bills will be taken care of. Leaving the extra gives you that necessary wiggle room for the occasional fluctuation in expenses. A suggested strategy for monthly bills is to set up autopayment where available but to periodically check that the amounts being deducted for each are as you expect, as companies tend to increase rates at random without letting you know. If you know you can't commit to checking periodically, then don't set up automatic bill pay. Prime candidates for autopay include rent, utilities, and insurance.

Spending checking account: This account is reserved for random or *fun* expenses. Include any subscriptions, such as movie/music streaming services, that are *not* required living expenses. This account will significantly help you stay on track if you allot exactly how much you're willing to spend on a monthly basis and *never* exceed it for *any* reason. This way, you'll maintain a sense of freedom in your leisure. We can still be real with ourselves while challenging the norm of careless spending. This account should have automatic payment deactivated if the service provider allows for it. It should hurt every time you need to draw from this account. Suggested items for this account include eating out, streaming services, drinking/partying, spontaneous big item purchases (monthly), entertainment, and gym membership.

We move on now to savings accounts. As with checking, it's important to understand the distinctions. A quick internet search of best high-yield savings accounts locally and nationwide will provide you with great options that will give you a better APY than traditional brick-and-mortar banks.

Emergency fund savings account: This account should *not* be touched except for its token purpose. A common rule tells us to set aside three to six months of expenses in this account for the worst-case scenarios. Situations that require taking capital out of this account include loss of a job or large medical expenses. It's best to pay these expenses out of pocket from your regular savings/spending account when you can; you never know when an even greater emergency may arise. This account should be funded before all else. Only then can the allocation of savings be spread across your other interests.

Funding for the next three accounts depends on your long-term strategy and knowledge of investing. Being conservative, aggressive, or goal-oriented will help determine where you feel comfortable placing your funds. Once the emergency fund is secure, allocate your net income into the next three buckets.

Long-term savings account (conservative): This account is best suited to your conservative savings plan. The goal here is to continuously accumulate capital without risking it in the investment market. In 30-40 years, you should have accumulated a significant safety net in case your investments don't see the growth you expected. This should be your second-to-last resort when it comes to taking out money for big expenses.

Investment savings account (aggressive): This account can be further broken down into a money market account (20%), automatic portfolio account (50%), and investment account (30%). The distribution used is based solely on your comfort level with regard to each of the three account types. I'm not a financial advisor, and the stock market is far from my area of expertise, but I put a portion of my investment savings toward a money market account just in case there's a significant dip in the market that I want to take advantage of. My automatic portfolio account is a long-term play while acting like the stock market in the sense that I'm able to sell my investment at any moment and take my profits. My focus here is on index funds, especially those managing portfolios of the top stock market companies. I invest a consistent amount every month, regardless of what the market is doing. The remaining 30% stays in the investment savings account for future investments not related to the stock market, as I'm a big advocate of diversifying my investment portfolio. This includes small businesses I'd like to invest in, real estate opportunities, and loans I provide at a higher interest rate than I may receive from savings accounts.

Other savings account (goal-oriented): This account is set up for major purchases anticipated for the next 6-24 months. There might be multiple *other* savings accounts, depending on your savings goals. I'd suggest having a vacation account, a new-car account, a house purchase account, then set aside the amount of money you need to be in a good position to meet those goals in a realistic timeframe. As always, your long-term goals will determine whether such accounts are funded more than their conservative and aggressive counterparts.

By following and completing these steps within seven days, you'll be well on your way to living a more comfortable and financially literate lifestyle.

Keep in mind that your budget is an ever-evolving machine that needs constant maintenance and monitoring to ensure you're staying on track. The more energy you put into creating it, the less time and effort you'll spend on future updates or worrying whether you have enough capital to survive. A "Seven-day Budget" template is included in this book's Resources section.

Chapter 5: Networking

It's not what you know; it's who you know. This common adage still holds true. Some would never guess that I identify myself as an introvert. I've spoken on stage before a crowd of hundreds, randomly started conversations with strangers, and have landed nearly every job I've had since college through some form of networking. These facts don't eliminate the butterflies I get each time I'm speaking to a large group, to a woman of interest, or to someone about a potential business relationship. The one thing that compels me to overcome the challenges of being an introvert is the tremendous power networking brings to accomplishing my goals. In this chapter, I'll be walking through some strategies from my networking journey that you can use to embrace your inner introvert or, for the extrovert, push even further to meet your needs.

Opportunity by Effort: During my second year of college, I switched majors from computer science to pursue a Bachelor of Professional Accountancy (B.P.A.). I didn't know much about accounting, as made obvious by the questions I asked during class, and my professor was initially concerned about my ability to comprehend the material. Though I appreciated his concern, my constant questions came from a place of genuine interest in the material. Numbers and money had always fascinated me, and I wanted to learn as much about them as I could. When I scored 97 on the first test, my professor was almost comically happy for me.

Accounting is about rules and guidelines. By understanding those rules and guidelines, I was able to apply the study habits I'd learned from math to find the right formula. As long as I had that formula in place, I could be confident in my answers. This dynamic continued throughout the semester, leading the professor and me to develop a solid teacher-student relationship. I had the same professor the following year, with similar results. That same year, my third of college, I ran into him one day at a job fair. He introduced me to a certified public accountant (CPA) from a regional firm with which he was associated. During that conversation, they invited me to their office for a walkthrough and to meet some of the partners. I stayed in touch with them until it was time for graduation and was offered a job. Unfortunately, I didn't live up to their expectations and was taught yet another valuable life lesson. Previous successes aren't necessarily an indication of future success. We should treat every opportunity as if it might disappear at any moment. Just having an opportunity is a milestone in and of itself. Regardless of the outcome, I've continued to lead with effort.

Being part of a Community: During my five years of playing college football at the Division II level, I created some unbelievable connections with my teammates. Guys who were once my high school rivals became brothers by our senior year of college. We pushed, fought, and mentored each other through some of the most challenging times of our lives. After being let go from my accounting position, I focused on obtaining my CPA license so I would be more marketable for my next position. One evening, I ran into an old teammate and we spent some time catching up. I let him know I was studying for the CPA exam and was looking for jobs anywhere and everywhere. He was still in school but had a cousin who worked for one of the Big Four and said he'd introduce me to them once I passed my exams.

Knowing I was to take my last exam within the month, this news gave me an extra push to make it happen. I took the exam, passed, and immediately gave him a call. He was able to get me on the phone with his cousin. Though she no longer worked at the accounting firm, she was still in touch with the HR manager from their Detroit practice. She helped get my resume up to par and passed it along. A few days later, I received an email to set up a phone interview. The phone interview went well and led to a three-person interview at their office.

I never practiced so hard for an interview in my life. For context, the typical interview process for Big Four accounting firms at my level starts at the big-name universities and business schools. They require multiple rounds of interviews, and you're competing against hundreds of bright college students with excellent grades, internships, and volunteer work under their belts. That's not to say I didn't have qualities that would allow me to hold my own in that pool of candidates; only that my path wasn't as rigorous. After my in-person interview, I left feeling pretty confident, but then, in the hallway, I saw the final partner with whom I interviewed. When I gave him a casual, "See you later," he didn't respond.

The overanalytical part of me replayed that interaction the whole ride home, and I was sure I wasn't getting the job. I vowed then and there never to act that way again, though it wasn't as if I needed to compensate for something I'd done wrong in the interview. Imagine my surprise when, two days later, I got a call from the HR manager, who told me the firm was extending me an offer. It felt like I'd been holding my breath for the last 48 hours and was only now letting it out! Had my teammate not brokered the connection, I would never have even heard of this firm—or, for that matter, the Big Four. I never grew so much, both personally and professionally, as I did during those stressful 70-hour workweeks.

Being Direct: Sometimes, nothing beats directly approaching people of worth and knowing precisely what you want. Take an individual's time into consideration when starting these conversations. If I'm attending a private trainers' networking event, for instance, and spotted the top-rated Boston-based trainer, I'm not going to bore him with details about my next vacation to Bora Bora with my puppy. This is where the so-called elevator pitch comes into play. After initial greetings and the opportunity presents itself, be prepared with a one to two-line statement about who you are, how you can help an individual, and your intentions. This is most effective when used in "speed networking" situations in which you'd like to meet a lot of people in a short period of time. When speaking about my online training service, I give variations of the following, depending on my audience:

I've created a centralized platform for sports and position-specific training that will help push athletes beyond their current skill level. This platform brings various levels of expertise across the country to one location without the hassle of digging through cute dog and baby videos on the internet to find it.

I like to break the ice with a bit of humor while making it clear that I have a viable (and valuable) product. The short-and-sweet approach accomplishes two things. First, it intrigues your audience. Second, it gives the listener time to consider leveraging your content for their own use or even becoming directly involved.

Actively Listen: Being direct is a great quality to have, but listening and responding to others' needs and concerns can help build rapport when one doesn't want to dominate the conversation. Listening tends to be an introvert's biggest asset, but extroverts can learn and benefit from it as well. If you're someone who doesn't feel the need to fill the air with words or be the center of attention, embrace that quality by listening and asking probing questions. By showing genuine interest, they'll be more likely to remember you over the countless others who babbled on and on about their own accomplishments. I do my best to give quality eye contact and full attention in every interaction—a skill I gained from tough football coaches who demanded nothing less. Keep in mind, however, that not all cultures appreciate direct eye contact.

Being Generous: I once worked in an office with an onsite fitness center. A lot of my peers look up to me when it comes to fitness, as I do my best to take care of myself. I typically charge $40-$60 for one-on-one training, but I also give away a lot of training for free, as I'm encouraged by others' motivation. We must remember we're all human beings and that it's okay to do something out of sheer kindness, keeping our minds off our wallets for once. Whenever I find out that coworkers have fitness goals, I always give them an opportunity to work out together and motivate each other. In addition to the motivational benefits I receive by having a workout partner, they benefit from training with an experienced individual. It's a win-win. Some people think I'm joking when I make the offer; others take me up on it without hesitation. In one particular case, a coworker in my department started joining me during my lunch workouts. We were consistent for around two months before lunch meetings started interfering. The results were amazing for both of us, and because of our different levels of experience, we knew to pace ourselves and not compete with each other. He eventually recommended me as a private trainer to his nephew, who was already an exceptional football player at the age of 10. We scheduled three workouts together, which led to future sessions and group training with his teammates. I neither expected nor initiated this connection. Simply being open to helping someone else opened doors for me that I wouldn't have had a chance to open otherwise. This strategy works just as well in business, as you'll see when we discuss my private training marketing strategy later in this book.

Try and Try Again: You can be a social butterfly, give away free products/services daily, say yes to every opportunity that comes up, and still not obtain the results you desire. This is an unfortunate truth about the journey of networking. For all the success stories I could share, I can recall many more instances in which the same approach led nowhere. I've learned not to dwell on how others react to my networking. The only thing I have control over is myself. I've been able to develop "tough skin" when it comes to rejection and failure through my continuous efforts to improve in this area. Some things come more naturally to me than others. It's up to me to adjust my input accordingly. With practice and consistency, networking will bring the desired results. At the very least, you'll be able to say you've grown and given back for a greater good.

That's the way life should be.

Chapter 6: Peer-to-peer Lending

I always felt destined to be a banker. Anytime I played Monopoly as a kid, I just *had* to be the banker. It just wasn't the same if I couldn't keep all the capital in order. My high win rate may also have something to do with being the banker, but that's a story for another book. Being the banker as a young adult, however, holds a lot more risk. While adjusting to this responsibility in the real world, I looked into peer-to-peer companies. Peer-to-peer lending is a type of crowdfunding that allows individuals access to unsecured loans for anything from student loan debt to the purchase of a new boat at competitive interest rates. On the flip side, lenders receive a competitive ROI in comparison to CDs, savings accounts, or other likeminded investment strategies. This crowdfunding style of lending was new to me, so before I dumped all of my money into being a lender, I had to learn what I liked and didn't like about this particular investment strategy.

My Portfolio:

I started investing through peer-to-peer lending companies in February 2015: a total of 29 notes at $25 apiece. Each loan had to be in multiples of $25, with $25 being the minimum. I was able to generate a net annualized return (NAR) of approximately 7.3% over the duration of having these loans. The NAR takes into consideration actual return less service fees, charge-offs, etc. The weighted average interest rate of the loans that I provided was approximately 8.5%. So, in turn, I paid 1.2% in fees to generate this revenue stream.

How it Works (Lender's Perspective):

Loans are graded based on a risk/reward scale. Certain companies use a letter scale in which an "A" grade is less risky and less rewarding, while an E grade is riskier and more rewarding, with a range of degrees in the middle (e.g., A2, A4, C5, D1). Many factors can impact the grade of the note, but listed below are some of the key factors I considered.

Grade: I never took on any notes that graded lower than a B. My notes were evenly spread across the varying A and B grades, with B1 loans taking the lion's share of my portfolio at 21%.

Employment length: I wanted to make sure my notes had a proven history of job security, so 38% of my note portfolio was made up of individuals with an employment length of 10+ years.

Type of loan: Debt consolidation accounted for 48% of my loan portfolio, while home improvements accounted for 21%. My rationale was that people who are thinking about debt consolidation and who are making an effort to improve their financial situation are likely to be more responsible. Home improvements showed me that the individual valued their property and would, therefore, be more responsible about paying.

FICO score: The FICO scores within my portfolio ranged from 665-824, with the average being 750. I considered FICO scores that were similar to mine and put a lot of personal weight on the fact that higher FICO scores translate into more responsibility.

Income: The ability to pay off a due balance is heavily derived from the amount of income being brought in. The average income of my portfolio was approximately $93,000, with over 90% of individuals having an income greater than $50,000.

Revolving debt utilization: As great as a high income is, I considered the revolving debt utilization (credit card debt to available balance ratio) more heavily. I know many individuals who, despite their large salaries, are living paycheck to paycheck and losing a lot of money on credit card interest because their balances never go away. Based on what creditors look for in credit card utilization, I didn't want to consider many loans with the utilization of greater than 30%. Approximately 65% of my portfolio had a debt utilization ratio of less than 30%. If that seems overwhelming, you can automate the selection process based on your risk appetite by either evenly spreading between grade levels or presetting the grade levels you wish to focus on. Regardless of whether you automate your funding or manually select it, you'll be able to see the suggested ROI you may receive. As investors, we must always be conscious that a forecasted return may not turn out that way, as we must rely on individuals to take care of their end. All we can do is monitor our investments and make timely adjustments as needed.

Thoughts on This Opportunity:

About a year into my peer-to-peer lending experience, I realized that my strategy wasn't as conservative as I thought. Considering that I was only receiving a 7.3% ROI, I wasn't generating enough gains to weather any type of significant charge off or default if it happened too early. One charge-off at $25 dollars would've wiped out much of my earnings. The only way to turn this investment into a truly conservative one was to diversify the grade of notes I took on. To incorporate more note diversification, the peer-to-peer lending company suggested a minimum balance of $5,000 to start. At the time, I wasn't comfortable putting $5,000 into peer-to-peer lending, let alone taking on notes that were below A or B ratings. All of these factors led me to discontinue my recurring investment and look for other strategies to capitalize on. I'm thankful that the one write-off that did take place didn't result in a significant loss; otherwise, I'd be sharing this story as one of learning without gain. Should I ever involve myself in peer-to-peer lending or crowdfunding again, I'd consider a real estate investment trust (REIT) or real estate-specific crowdfunding opportunities that do significantly more vetting.

Chapter 7: Private Training and Marketing

"Be the person you needed when you were growing up."

This phrase stuck with me throughout college and continues to inspire me in my professional career. You might say it was the seed for this very book. In high school and college, I played wide receiver on the football team and was presented starting/key roles early in my career. I was considered to be one of the top players in my position. As cool as it was to be looked at as a leader at such a young age (we typically had a young receiving core), I yearned for that one upperclassman leader to tell me, "You're good but not great. Here's what you'll need to get there." By my senior year of college, I accepted that lack of guidance, mentorship, and brotherhood and took it upon myself to become that leader, both for myself and others striving for that same success.

This hunger to help others came with its own complications. When I started reaching out to give guidance to my peers or younger cousins, I was merely forcing their dreams, not the other way around. At that point, the advice was free and easily tossed aside. It wasn't until I created a profile on an online sports platform, connecting players and coaches in specific areas, that I started finding people who were *really* hungry for success.

My First Client

My original goal was to find one athlete I could mentor and show what it takes to be successful. I finally got that first client at $15 per session (platform minimum) and we scheduled a session within the first week of booking. I was so excited that I almost couldn't hold it in. I spent the whole week setting up the perfect game plan, pondering the advice I was going to give him, and envisioning how perfect this journey was going to be. But in the first five minutes following our warm-up, he rolled his ankle and couldn't run anymore. To say I thought I was the worst private trainer in the world would be the understatement of the century. All I'd done was ask him to demonstrate how he'd run a five-yard stop route (hitch) without initial instruction. He seemed athletic enough to handle it, but clearly, the universe was playing a mean joke on me. Seeing that he'd hurt himself, I asked if he wanted to continue. He tried to run, but to no avail, then tried squatting and nearly fell to the ground. I shifted focus to his catching, as I'd noticed that his form was off when throwing the ball around just prior to starting practice. He agreed, and we spent the next 45 minutes catching the football from various angles and talking about specifics of hand placement. Somehow, we were able to make the workout productive and leave on a good note. I was still nervous about how things turned out and thought I would need to find another client to train with. A few days later, when I thought my coaching career was over for sure, I received a notification that an additional five sessions had been booked. I nearly jumped through the roof. Five sessions later, the father of this athlete left me a review. Hands sweating and heart racing, I impatiently waited for the website to load:

> *Coach Andrew is very professional, great at explaining and demonstrating important skill techniques, very focused. I have seen an improvement in my son's skill and confidence level during each session with Coach Andrew. I highly recommend this coach.*

As fast as my emotional rollercoaster dropped on that first session, that was a snail's pace compared to its joyful rise upon reading this review. I had secured my first student; he was growing and his father saw the value I was bringing. I was starting to believe I was on to something. Sadly, this part of the journey had to end after 10 sessions, when I was sent out of state on an external audit assignment that lasted throughout football season until I relocated to Massachusetts. Little did I know that this move would take my personal training to the next level.

Expanding My Client Base:

Officially settled in Massachusetts, I was gaining exposure through my online training business, high ratings/reviews, and word of mouth from my athletes. My goal was to develop not only their abilities but also their character as young adults who would flourish and excel in anything they put their minds to. This approach landed me as the site's #2 ranked football coach in Massachusetts. Beyond my coaching abilities, I propelled my ranking by first setting up a quality profile in which I laid out my experience, accolades, and game plan. That way, every potential client could see what I was about and the athletic journey I'd taken to get to this point. I made sure to keep my profile honest because the last thing I wanted was for a client to expect something I couldn't produce. For example, I'd never trained offensive/defensive linemen and made it a point to exclude those position groups from my experience. I also provided pictures and videos of my training so that my energy and passion would shine through. Second, I priced my services to the market. Some would say always charge what (you think) you're worth, but I believe in establishing a proven track record of clients first before attempting to charge your true value. Once you've proven yourself in the market, the price will set itself.

Over my five years developing athletes in the sport that I love, I managed to obtain 40 clients, generate over $12,000 in gross profits, get involved in promotional banners/events, and make some everlasting relationships. As much as I grew as a private trainer, there came the point where I needed to take client acquisition into my own hands and set myself apart. This journey taught me a valuable lesson in effort and patience. And so, on December 15, 2016, I started reaching out to 15-30 athletes a day and offering one free 90-minute group training. I required each athlete to fill out a liability waiver in case of injury and a profile sheet to track who was attending. After the first free session, it cost $15 to participate. Keep in mind this was during the winter and temperatures were close to freezing on some days. My first group session started with five athletes, three of whom I already knew.

As I stayed consistent with my outreach and posting content from my workouts, the numbers grew and grew. By weeks 7-9, we had 14-17 athletes competing against each other. Focus and energy were sky high, and athletes left each workout exhausted but hungry for more.

The Downfall

I was extremely happy with the growth I was seeing, but certain factors led me to end these group trainings.

Lack of consistency: My social media outreach dropped from 15-30 daily to 10-12 every other day. By not consistently reaching out to new athletes and providing free training, I wasn't able to keep my numbers up. I should've continued reaching out to 15-30 athletes daily for at least a year or until I was able to build enough traction for athletes to find me more consistently. Customer outreach should never falter. It might not come from you directly, but building clients is a key part of a business and will always fuel your growth.

Unclear messaging: When I originally sent out invites to athletes, I let them know about myself, the training I was putting together, the dates and times, and that the training was free to attend. This worked well enough, and the athletes showed up. What I failed to mention was that the training was only free that *one time*. It wasn't until they met me in person that they found out it wasn't free beyond that. I'd built up excitement, only to throw it back in their face without ever meaning to. Had I been upfront about the fees and let each athlete know exactly what to expect, they would've learned to trust me from the get-go. I did eventually change my messaging to include full disclosure about future costs, but I'd already lost potential clients early on from lack of clarity.

Greedy marketing strategy: I pride myself on providing as much content for free as possible until people are almost begging to buy from me. If only I'd followed my own advice this time as well. The sessions weren't consistently packed with people asking me to join. Depending on your financial position, it's best to leverage as much in the way of freebies as possible. I saw the money potential of these workouts and got too eager to obtain it.

As my outreach declined, so did the number of attendees—from 17 to 12 to 5 and, ultimately, zero. I fell away from the scene for over a year before sticking to my plan by providing value first and allowing the benefits to come as they may. Which was the overall goal from the beginning. I missed out on an untapped market by not being consistent, patient, or focused on the long-term objective. This is something I don't plan on letting happen ever again.

Chapter 8: Credit Card Churning

I'd like to take you through my journey of making over $4,000 in free money within a nine-month span by capitalizing on sign-up bonuses. Otherwise known as credit card churning, this strategy is open to any responsible credit card user with a proven record of maintaining multiple accounts.

I stumbled upon credit card churning by chance while looking for nontraditional ways to make additional money. At first, I'd been seeking a high-yield interest rate in which to house my money but wasn't satisfied with the mere 2-2.35% APY I was being offered at the time. I scoured the internet for the best checking/savings sign-up bonuses and put together a list of potential candidates. Even though I wouldn't be capitalizing on every account, especially because some were region-specific, I wanted to have this list available for friends living in those areas who might wish to take advantage in the future. I started light, signing up for three checking accounts for a total of $725 dollars in bonus cash.

After opening these accounts, I looked into credit card churning for additional bonus opportunities and was excited by what I found. I started credit card churning with a credit score of 775, which allowed me to get approved for sixteen accounts (eight checking/savings and eight credit cards). After opening my first credit card, my credit availability increased, thus boosting my credit score to 792. I expected this score to fluctuate, as it didn't take into consideration further accounts opened later on during this nine-month period.

Making the Right Decisions

To determine which credit cards I signed up for, I ranked them in accordance with the following criteria:

What is the Return on the Opportunity?

Return on the opportunity, or ROO, is the cashback I'd be receiving for the amount of money I had to spend. Ideally, I was looking for a ROO of 15% or more of the amount I had to spend on my credit card. For example, one of my credit cards offered a $500 return after spending at least $3,000 within the first three months: a 16.67% return. For comparison, another credit card required $2,500 of spending to receive $150 (a 6% ROO). The latter wasn't worth the effort. By the end of this credit card churning period, I concluded that those credit cards providing the highest dollar return were also the most beneficial, as credit cards have a hard pull on your credit report, which limits how many cards you can apply for in the long run.

Is there an annual fee?

a) If yes, is there an introductory free period?

i) If yes again, I cancel the card before the annual fee is charged.

ii) If no, I don't sign up for the card, as it would cut into my profits. Even if the profit would be substantial, I remind myself that I'm trying to be as conservative as possible.

b) If there is no annual fee, is there an interest-free period?

i) If yes, I pay the minimum balance until the interest-free period is over, then pay the remaining statement balance in full. Note that whenever I hit the spend requirement, I stop using this card. It's easy to think about taking advantage of all the interest-free money, but doing so would add additional risk of default/non-payment that I'm not willing to take on.

ii) If there is no interest-free period, I set up an auto-payment of the statement balance so that no interest fee is ever charged to me.

Regarding checking/savings accounts, the following criteria aided in my decision to apply.

Location of the promotion: Certain promos are city- and/or state specific. I typically start with an internet search for checking/savings promotions in my state.

Hard vs. soft pull: A hard and soft pull look at the same information with regard to a consumer's credit responsibility. This includes the number of accounts opened, tax liens, history of on-time payments, collections, etc. The difference between the two relates to whether the individual in question has inquired about borrowing money. Since checking/savings accounts are not opened to borrow money, they're not likely to incur a hard pull on your credit. Before applying for an account, I always checked with the bank directly to ensure the account was a soft pull. If your focus is on checking/saving accounts, denial may happen less frequently since the report to your credit doesn't include a hard pull. Keep in mind that you're still opening a new account. This will impact your credit regardless of the type of pull.

Minimum deposit/balance required: Many of the accounts I opened required some type of direct deposit from a job, dividends, disability payments, and/or government deposits. In most cases, I used my job income to take care of high direct deposit requirements. When I started to stretch my direct deposit thin, I diversified my direct deposit payments from the short-term rental and coaching earnings across various accounts. With a recurring deposit, it's important to understand the various time frames involved here. Some banks require a set amount directly deposited each month for a number of months, while others simply require you to make at least a minimum direct deposit within the first two months. On top of direct deposits, some banks require a minimum balance in the account for three to six months. I look to capitalize on accounts with high cash bonuses that require no (or low) minimum balances. This maximizes my return in the manner of a glorified savings account. If I can leave $25 in my account for six months and remove it, I will. The fine print here is, of course, *very* important. Some banks state that it takes three months to earn the advertised bonus but that you must keep the account open for *six* months or fees will be charged.

Required transactions: Accounts that require a minimum number of monthly transactions are the ones I shy away from the most (and the ones that have undermined my bonus most often). These are usually checking accounts that provide a debit card. One must pay close attention to the types of transactions being counted toward the promotion. Always read the fine print.

Monthly fees: This might seem like an automatic deal-breaker, but it really depends on whether the fees can be waived or the cash bonus is substantial enough. Banks may waive fees if you have an average daily balance over a certain amount, set up a monthly direct deposit, or use the card a certain number of times per month. When a bank does not waive the fees, I calculate my return less the monthly fee and cancel the account as soon as possible.

Return on investment (ROI): I also looked at the ROI I was getting for the amount of money I had to give up. To truly understand my ROI, I took whatever ROI I was receiving for that time period and annualized that number. For example, one account I opened offered a $300 sign-up bonus for a minimum deposit of $2,500 and required that I keep that money in the account for 60 days to receive the bonus. And once those 60 days had passed, it would take an additional 30 days for the money to be deposited into my account. It's worth noting, too, that the account could be closed at any time without penalty after the deposit was received. This meant I wouldn't have access to my money for a quarter of a year. The ROI percentage of $300 for a deposit of $2,500 was 12%. Since it only took me three out of the 12 months in the year to generate this profit, I was able to multiply that 12% by 4 to determine an annualized profit of 48% and...show me a faster and safer way to earn a 48% ROI, and I'll be there in a heartbeat! I then opened another account offering a $400 sign-up bonus for a minimum deposit of $25, a direct deposit of $1,000 per month, and one transaction per month. The payout occurred after maintaining the account for 90 days, and the account could be closed at any time without penalty. This translated into a 1600% ROI (6400% annualized), given that only $25 was required as a minimum deposit.

Overall, I focus on minimum balances and how much activity and/or movement is required across the above criteria. I always start with the most advantageous account, then work down my list until I've closed each in a timely manner. Closing may not sound too appealing, but if the bank decides to provide other offers in the future, you may still be eligible if enough time has elapsed since you were last an active account holder. I've seen that requirement in the range of 12 to 18 months of not being an account holder for some institutions.

Possible Roadblocks

Slow application acceptance due to multiple accounts being opened at once: After applying for 13 cards within a span of six months, I was denied for a checking and credit card account. The credit card was high profile, so denial in that instance was understandable. The checking account denial, however, was a bit shocking, as checking accounts only do soft pulls of your credit history.

Having to be cognizant of the requirements for each account: Whether due to hidden fees or your own negligence, it can be easy to miss out on the perk if not careful. In one instance, I missed out on $300 for neglecting to read the fine print. This particular checking account required me to make 10 debit card purchases within the first two months. After making 14 payments, I checked the account, expecting to receive my bonus, only to be informed by customer service that only nine of the required transactions were debit card purchases. I closed the account right away and gave them an earful of my displeasure over their services, even though the fault was entirely my own.

Having to report all checking/savings account gains on taxes: Banks consider payments to be as interest received for tax purposes. Credit card sign-up bonuses are points and therefore, tax-exempt. In my case, this resulted in $1,850 being taxed.

Credit score fluctuation: My credit score rose and fell between 50 and 60 points over the period I was opening new accounts (a negative), gaining credit availability (a positive), and increasing my consumer debt balance by not paying off all credit cards right away (another negative). This fluctuation worried me after the initial drop, but with consistency and prompt payments, that score shot right back up.

Having enough capital in each account: At any given time, I might've had four different checking/savings accounts open at once, each requiring its own minimum balance or direct deposit. Accounts requiring direct deposit were typically checking, and I had no interest in keeping my money in such accounts with low annual percentage yields (APYs), so I made quite frequent transfers into my high-yield savings account. The minimum balance requirements limited my investment flexibility, as ignoring them would've incurred monthly fees or start the three-month waiting period all over again. After putting $5,000 into one such account, where it was to sit untouched, I accidentally made a payment out of that account, mistaking the debit card associated with it for another one that looked very similar. I was able to cancel the payment from the vendor's side and get my money back, but from the bank's perspective, the damage was already done. My bonus cycle restarted and I had to wait another three months before getting the bonus paid out. Thankfully, this account didn't have a monthly fee minimum balance requirement.

Conclusion

The typical strategy here is to credit card churn only when you know you have big expenses coming up. That way, you aren't sustaining consistent hits to your credit report and are taking advantage of extended interest-free periods. The short-term benefits of earning over $4,000 with only a seven-point drop in my credit score spoke for themselves. While juggling those accounts wasn't too much of a time commitment, I had to keep my mind sharp to avoid careless mistakes. Had I continued credit card churning for six more months, the approval process would've gotten tougher. If I could do it all over again, I'd initially focus only on checking/savings accounts that do soft pulls of credit scores before shifting my attention to high-yield credit cards to minimize the number of accounts for which I needed approval.

Chapter 9: Short-term Rental Income

The $1,700 Decision

For a 756-square-foot 2-bedroom, 1-bathroom apartment (including utilities) in Framingham, Massachusetts, I paid $1,700 per month. Keep in mind that Framingham is 30-45 minutes outside of Boston, depending on traffic. Recently single and locked into an annual lease I had no business being in, I was stuck trying to figure out a way to build on my financial goals without rent draining my pockets every month.

My Options

Move: It's easy to think that moving back home, where I could easily find a comparable apartment closer to the city for $800-$1,200, would be the perfect situation. I'd be closer to family and friends, and saving would be the least of my worries. But I firmly believe that everything happens for a reason and the opportunities being presented to me in New England outweighed the comfort of being back in Michigan.

Move-in with someone else: I ruled out this option from the beginning because my apartment was fully furnished in exactly the way I wanted it to be. I wasn't about to give up any of my furniture to make room for someone else's or watch as people (mis)treated my things like their own.

Get a roommate: In addition to issues of space and personal property, I've had terrible roommate experiences, ranging from non-payment to dishes littered across every inch of counter space, and even eating all of my food without asking! (And anyone who knows me knows how much I *love* my food.) I just wasn't willing to risk my peace of mind for a long-term roommate. I even considered month-to-month terms through sites like Roomster and Roommates.com but gained little traction.

Rent out my room through a short-term rental platform: Living in Framingham, I never expected short-term rental to be a viable option. Being the quiet family town that it is, Framingham seemed a far cry from the luxury urban apartments I'd always associated with short-term rentals. But then I had a lunch meeting with a friend who told me about her flourishing short-term rental business, which catered to the many business people who came to the area for work. This was enough to convince me to give it a try.

Why a Short-term Rental?

Short-term stays: The typical stay for my Framingham apartment was between 1.5 weeks to 1.5 months. I took comfort in knowing that even if I didn't like the guest's personality or cleanliness, they'd be gone soon enough.

Income potential: While doing my initial research, I learned that a shared living space similar to mine was earning approximately $25-$50 per day or $750-$1,500 per month. I took a conservative approach, listing my place for around $30-$40 to encourage more bookings. This meant a potential income of $900-$1,100 per month. Interestingly enough, I was on the frugal end of things and only provided a king-size blowup mattress that cost me $60. Knowing what I know now, I would've spent the extra money to provide more comfortable sleeping arrangements and upped my price accordingly. Refer to "The Numbers" below for full details.

Guest ratings: My first short-term rental experience took place during a trip to Utah with a coworker. Not knowing any better, I thought of it like a hotel where you didn't necessarily have to put things back in place. My coworker quickly disowned me of that illusion, as he had an excellent rating and didn't want to mess that up. Remembering this experience made me feel comfortable that other guests would have the same mindset. This proved to be true., as most guests were very apologetic about their noise levels and any "mess" they made. Most of the time, the guest room looked like nobody was ever there.

Cons of Short-term Rentals

Guest preferences: Some guests expect five-star services for $30 a night. It's an unfortunate truth that you cannot please everybody, no matter how much you try. It's also true that the guest is always right, and it's the host's job to ensure that everyone is satisfied. In the example below, you'll see how I responded to one guest's knocking off a star for not having a microwave.

Jan 17 - Jan 19 . $36
Framingham private room with parking
★★★★☆

Public feedback

Great place, lots of things to play around. Host is cool. However, just a note, there is no microwave oven, in case you expect one.

Public response

Thank you for the feedback. Although I did not specify having a microwave in my apartment, I have since added a microwave if this ever becomes a necessity. Nonetheless, I was happy to have you stay at my unit.

Taxes: As with all miscellaneous income, you can be sure the government will want their cut. How well you research your market and track your expenses will determine if Uncle Sam is going to hurt your margins. To be conservative, I kept a 28% reserve in my savings to be ready for any tax payments. In any case, consult with your tax specialist for specifics on short-term rental taxes.

Landlord clearance: As a renter, you *must* get clearance from your landlord before offering your place for short-term rentals. Without that clearance, you run the risk of breaking your lease and kissing any good recommendations for future apartments goodbye. Owning your own property would obviously eliminate this issue.

The Numbers

Below you'll find a numerical breakdown of short-term rental versus roommate for my Framingham apartment. A few things to note:

a) The short-term rental period was from 15 January 2018 to 1 November 2018,
b) Taxes and/or deductions are not included,
c) Heat and water were paid for by the landlord. Ultimately, I ended up paying the same or slightly less than with a roommate, but with a lot more peace of mind and a clean apartment!

	Short-Term Rental		Roommate	
Rent	$	(1,550)	$	(1,550)
Utilites		(42)		(42)
Cable		(100)		(100)
Heat/Water	$	-	$	-
Total Expenses	$	(1,692)	$	(1,692)
Income	$	952	$	846
Net Income (Rent)	$	(740)	$	(846)

Short-term Rental: The Sequel

Considering how well my short-term rental did in Framingham, I was excited to take this strategy to a condo in Dorchester, MA (a neighborhood of Boston) to fully embrace my goal of becoming a true Bostonian. Little did I know how different the market would be. The following are some key differences.

Guests demographic shift: While Framingham brought in many business travelers looking for short-term stays, stays for my Boston guests have consistently ranged from 2-10 days. Guests are usually on vacation or checking out potential schools in the city. In just two months, I've been able to meet people from across the world with different backgrounds and interests in the city.

Higher rent: My rent instantly shot up from $1,700 all-in to approximately $2,200 all-in for no other reason than being in the city (and not even the heart of the city, for that matter). Knowing I wanted to live near the city, I was willing to pay more money for the experience, though my ultimate goal was to leverage my short-term rental so as to cover my rent fully. The higher rent forced me to be creative with the furnishing of my condo. Beyond the dining table, couch, and TV stand, I was able to purchase all furniture for under $500 (including the bed, bed-frame, and TV itself). Who knew that secondhand shopping was my superpower?

More competition: Given the number of multi-family apartments and large homes in Boston, the market is highly competitive and has required me to do things to set myself apart. The air mattress in the bedroom just doesn't cut it anymore.

Higher income potential: Because Boston is a tourist city, the income potential for shared spaces is, of course, much higher than Framingham. During the peak season of summer, my unit jumped from a monthly gross average of $1,200 to $2,700. I wouldn't have believed this to be true if people weren't already booking my condo for July at the increased rates. I expect to average approximately $1,700 from this condo for the current year, which will put a nice dent into my rent expense.

Conclusion

Since hopping on the short-term rental bandwagon, for starters, I've enjoyed how clean my apartment has been compared to living without guests. I enjoy the interactions with new people and getting to understand different lifestyles. I also enjoy the extra money going into my pocket on a monthly basis. Renting out my space has motivated me to look into owning property and capitalizing on the lower mortgage cost compared to rents priced to make a profit for landlords.

Chapter 10: Purchasing Investment Properties

Purchasing investment properties all began when I noticed a friend sharing pictures on social media of a real estate deal he was involved in. I asked him how I might get involved until he finally let me join in on rehabbing his home, which despite being paid off in full, needed additional capital for the rehab. He offered me 15% on $15,000 for a three-month loan. The rehab ended up going beyond three months and required additional capital, which I provided at a 10% rate. This caused a bit of confusion, as the contract never specifically laid out terms for additional capital. Had he not been a personal friend, we might've parted on bad terms, but we were able to work through the disagreement like professionals. It was a great learning experience for both of us. Once the house was sold, I received my principal plus interest, and my friend was a happy man. The downfall of being an angel investor, taking a percentage of capital over equity, was that the profit margin on the house ended up being significantly higher than what I made on my onetime investment. I knew the potential to make more was there. I also knew I was more assured of a return by a set date, whereas my friend was in the riskier position of having to sell the house for more than what he'd put into it. Regardless of how well it sold, I was entitled to 15%. Moreover, this experience was a litmus test to see how well we might work together on future projects. Given the project's success, we decided to move on with another investment opportunity.

The First House Investment

Three months after my friend closed on his house, he was ready to dive into the foreclosure auction circuit in search of more properties to sell. We found a promising one in Detroit, Michigan, close to the University of Detroit Mercy. Prior to starting his own venture, my friend (now business partner) had brokered real estate deals in the city of Detroit for more than eight years under his father. He had an amazing ability to uncover deals in properties that others wouldn't touch. Well aware of his track record, I was impressed enough to let him spearhead the process. I happily took on the role of both capital investor and student. Outside of looking to generate a significant profit within a year, I hoped to gain a better understanding of real estate so that I might expand and branch off on my own someday. What follows is our process from start to finish.

Signing the Contract

Once my friend and I decided to become business partners, we made it official by drawing up the terms of the contract. We understood from our previous experience that having all the particulars laid out would be vital, regardless—if not especially because—of our friendship. Key terms laid out in the agreement included Equity Split, Cost Split, and Exit Strategy. The actual terms are listed below.

Andrew Beaver
Expenses:
- 50% Split

Sale Proceeds:
- 45% of net profits

Responsibility:
- 50% cost

Rental Proceeds:
- 50% of rental income

Business Partner
Expenses:
- 50% Split

Sale Proceeds:
- 55% of net profits

Rental Proceeds:
- 50% of rental income

Responsibility:
- Finds and purchases property
- Manages contractors
- Manages the sale of property

My business partner wanted to split the profits 50/50, but given the disproportionate amount of effort on his part, I believed it was only right to give additional equity to cover the property management.

The LLC

Next, we established a limited liability company, or LLC, through which we could funnel revenue and expenses. Our goal in establishing an LLC was to limit any personal liability in the event that something went wrong with the property. We also wanted to explicitly separate business and personal expenses to avoid confusion come tax time. We set up a separate bank account to which we both had access. I was able to see when money left the account and for what reason, if not already communicated to me. I didn't spend a lot of time monitoring the account because as a silent investor there must be *some* level of trust while I focus on growing my other business ventures.

Research

After the LLC was established, we set about finding our property. Knowing the auction was approximately a month away, we had time to get a full list together of the properties we wanted to bid on. The auction site lists properties from owners who either neglected to pay their mortgage for a few months or haven't paid their property taxes. These properties can be purchased at a significant discount compared to what is actually owed on the property. The city of Detroit provides a listing of all these properties, along with such information as the bedroom/bathroom count, date built, and address. Pictures aren't always available, and in any case, it's best to see the property in person. This isn't always possible, as the original owner may still reside there or the property may be off-limits, which can compound the risks. If city officials catch you trespassing on someone else's property, you might find yourself in a lot of trouble.

To make a shortlist, we first narrowed down our properties of interest to those that met our target criteria. Our demographic of choice was families looking for a 3 bedroom, 1 to 1½ bathroom house with approximately 1300 square feet of space. Based on our research of sell prices in the areas we were looking at, we knew this would give us a consistently good return. After filtering for these items, my partner drove out to each property multiple times to cut the list down. What began as a list of well over two hundred properties eventually narrowed down to ten. I flew into town to join in on some of the drive-throughs and to ensure we agreed on which houses we were targeting, all the while gaining valuable firsthand experience.

Strategies from the Field

Throughout this process, we capitalized on a number of strategies to keep as much skin in the game as possible. One option we kept in our back pocket at all times was to offer the current owner the option of letting us pay off their taxes and purchasing the house outside of the auction. This is one way of preserving a bit of a relationship with the original owner and potentially decreasing the purchase price. Other key considerations with regard to properties are as follows.

Proximity to the highway: We were considerate of commuters who needed access to the main highways but didn't want to deal with the noise pollution of living directly off the highway.

Proximity to schools: Because our target market revolved around families, being close to a reputable school district was important. Being close to a university was an added bonus.

Specific neighborhoods/streets: Given Detroit's history and crime rates, which vary from neighborhood to neighborhood (and even street to street), it was important to have a deep understanding of which parts to avoid. This was where my partner's expertise came into play and where many investors fall short. A house in and of itself might show significant upside, but if the entire street doesn't come with that same promise, the house's value is sure to diminish. My partner picked a majority of deals this way because the Detroit market at the time was swarming with predatory investors snatching up properties in hopes the market would turn around regardless of street conditions. In most cases, such investors ended up putting those properties back on the market and selling at significant losses — a naïve way to do business.

Conditions of surrounding properties: A good rule of thumb to follow is to spend time on the multiple listing service (MLS) or auction listings to figure out what properties fit your initial criteria, then drive out to these properties to get a better sense of the neighborhood and surroundings. If the house next to your potential investment property is abandoned or in poor condition, your property's overall value will do down. If the neighborhood is clean and well kept, that's a sign the immediate community cares about their homes and upkeep. Be sure to refer to the MLS to determine the selling price of neighboring houses for comparison.

Comparables: Without knowing the exact condition of a house, determining comparables can be a challenge. Based on the criteria listed above, and by leveraging online travel agencies, agents, etc., we were able to determine a range as to what a property would sell for and a possible purchase price (including repair cost). To determine your comparable properties, filter the MLS for properties sold (preferably) within the last three months. If a property hasn't been sold within the last three months in your desired neighborhood, consider whether there might be something you should be concerned about and/or expand your search to six or nine months. The most recently sold properties in our neighborhood of interest had gone for anywhere between $45,000 and $75,000, depending on whether the property was rehabbed. Recently listed rehabbed properties were listed in the $65,000-85,000 range, but we knew to consider that list range as secondary to the sold range. If a property wasn't going to generate us at least a $25,000 buffer between total cost and sell price, it wasn't even on our radar. We anticipated approximately $15,000-20,000 for a full rehab job on a property with a purchase price of around $10,000-25,000. In total, we were looking to fund $25,000-45,000 in cash. The goal was to sell the property within three months of purchase for around $70,000 to get us within our $25,000 profit range. This is how it all played out.

The Auction

We had our properties picked out, our maximum bid noted, and our popcorn in hand for a great show. Unfortunately, competition in these auctions is fierce. Given that the Detroit market has hit rock bottom, corporations are willing to overpay for properties and hold on to them until the local economy turns around. This hurts individual and small group investors like us who are playing the short-term game on a relatively limited budget. Six out of the 10 properties on our list went well over our budgeted amount. Of the remaining four, my partner picked up three while he and I went in together on the last one. We were happy to get the latter property for $22,000, which was just under our budgeted amount. I'd officially just purchased my first investment property! Now it was time to make some money. Or so we thought.

Before we could actually start working on the property, we needed the deed in hand and the now-former owner to move out. When we told the former owner that the property was no longer his, he refused to leave and requested that we provide him with the deed as proof that we owned the property. We purchased the property in October 2018. He didn't move out until January 2019, and only then at the last possible minute after we handed him an eviction notice. We tried to ease the situation by using a "cash for keys" strategy. We gave him money to help smooth the transition, and in return, he'd move out on time and not destroy the property. After finding out that he had roofing experience, we even offered him some work to build rapport. All was for nothing, however, as he kept putting things off and eventually stopped returning our calls. We were hoping to have the property fully renovated before the winter hit, but with such a long delay, our *Fix and Flip* project wasn't looking promising. The fact that we'd paid in cash meant we weren't losing money from interest, but timing is everything in real estate. Winter is one of the most difficult times to sell, even in a good market—let alone in Detroit, where homebuyers aren't exactly lining up at open houses the moment a place hits the market. The lack of action gave us plenty of time to come up with a contingency plan: We would put a tenant in the property to generate revenue and sell the property to an investor. Ideally, however, given the amount of work we'd put into it, we wanted a homebuyer, not a turnkey investment.

I was totally ignorant of this part of the process. It never occurred to me that in order to obtain a property, improve it, and make a profit from it, you actually had to uproot someone from their home and displace them elsewhere. For a moment, I battled with the realization that investors may not be the nicest individuals to deal with in these types of situations. I wanted to see myself as a genuinely nice guy in the business world, but being nice isn't always realistic.

The Costs of Rehab

Once December rolled around, and the former owner finally moved out, my partner got straight to work fixing up the place with his contractors. In light of the fact that someone had been living in it until recently, we knew that it was, at the very least, habitable. Our rehab cost came out to approximately $20,000, which meant $42,000 invested in total so far.

It took less than a month for all required repairs to be made and we were able to put the property on the market in February 2019 at $69,900 price point. Relieved at finally finishing the project within budget and one step closer to rolling in it, imagine my surprise when a week went by of interest but no offers. Then two weeks of the same. Then six. My partner gathered that the price point, in combination with the winter season, was working against us. We decided to take the property off of the market until the spring when people would be more inclined to purchase a home. We didn't want the stigma of having a property sitting on the market for too long, as buyers would likely start to wonder whether the property had some hidden issues. In April 2019, just as we were looking to put the property back on the market, we were met with another *friendly* surprise. The ceiling was leaking! By now, I was freaking out, especially in light of the money we'd put into the repairs. Thankfully, the leak was caused by a burst pipe rather than a broken roof—significantly reducing repair time (and the cost associated with it) to a mere week. In early May 2019, the property was listed on the MLS and ready to be sold at $64,900: a $5,000 reduction from the original asking price. We had to be honest with ourselves about our initial optimism and hoped the property would sell within the month.

Fast forward to August 2019, and the property still hadn't sold. At one point, we considered grouping the property as part of a package deal with others owned by my business partner. This would've brought the selling price down to $60,000, so we ultimately decided to keep the property and rent it out until its market value increased. We decided on placing Section 8 tenants into the property and were able to get a $1,200 payment per month approved by Section 8. It would take us approximately four years to recoup our investment (including tax payments) in full.

Overall, I was very pleased with the outcome of my first property investment adventure. I learned a lot through the experience, and it gave me the confidence to continue investing in the Detroit market as well as in smaller Boston suburbs. The amount of knowledge I gained through the challenges I faced outweighed the additional revenue I might've generated had the investment gone smoothly from the beginning. Generating passive income and increasing the value of a community is something I look forward to doing for many years to come.

Chapter 11: A Costly Life Lesson

Over half of new businesses fail within their first year. After eight months of tirelessly working on my online sports training platform, The Drill Factory, I was faced with the possibility of failure. As a personal trainer, I'm constantly looking to maximize workouts for my private clients, but I always found myself thinking, "Why is it so difficult to find quality training materials on the internet?" The fruitless search for such materials inspired me: I would find a way to store all of my workouts in one place while continuously building an online database of material that I could refer to anytime I needed a workout. Creating this database would help me minimize time spent searching for workouts later on. I started drawing out all the workouts that I currently had in mind, as well as others I'd found online, with the intention of one day making them into videos.

This database, I came to realize, had the potential to be of great help not only to me but also athletes worldwide who might not have access to their own trainer. In a stroke of naivety, I thought I could simply whip up the database using the small bit of savings I had, then share it for free. Sadly, the scope of my project required more capital than I anticipated. I mapped out the features I knew would be vital to the platform's success. I got them ready for initial discussions with a developer, thinking this would avoid small but costly changes in the platform development process down the road. I extensively researched my competitors, folding inspiration into the batter of what I'd begun to create: a visual outline of each page of my app. Though the wireframe wasn't "pretty," it effectively painted the picture of what I wanted. I had my heart set on a US-based company to develop the app but wasn't prepared for the cost tradeoffs that came with it.

The company in question quoted me nearly half a million dollars for the first version of my app. No, that's not a typo. *Five hundred thousand* dollars. I tried not to laugh when I said, "I'll think it over and call you back," quickly hanging up the phone. I was back to square one and needed to generate revenue somehow to offset the costs associated with building the platform. I widened my search to include international companies and the possibility of leveraging resources from India or Colombia. Any apprehension I had over working with an offshore team was due to bad experiences in the past, but I knew the low costs and faster turnaround times could outweigh any communication difficulties. Either way, I was equipped with a better understanding of my needs and how to stress the importance of frequent communication and updates. Once I found a company I thought had potential, I requested examples of their work, looked for recommendations, and searched for reviews from previous clients. Upon seeing my wireframe, the company owner demonstrated a clear understanding of what I wanted, so I felt secure in hiring him.

I asked the developer to send me a full quote that included everything I wanted for the platform. When I noticed that some components of my original wireframe were missing from the quote, he assured me even the smallest details would not be forgotten, and that anything missing would immediately be added at no additional cost. True to business form, I accepted this statement by adding a relevant clause to the contract. The total cost for the project came to approximately $36,000, with payments to be made in four $9,000 increments. In hindsight, this should've been a red flag due to how expensive it was, but at the time I thought that as long as they provided me with a functioning mobile app, I could always have it tweaked by a more established company later on for the next iteration.

The wireframing process of app development is typically a week-long process and not very costly. Even without experience, I was able to create a 40-page wireframe, displaying the registration and overall user process from scratch, in less than a week for a different project. The assigned technician took two months to create my wireframe. Though I will admit to being a perfectionist, I was very patient in working with this technician to ensure they fully understood and could deliver my vision. All the while, I was initiating talks, holding meetings, and requesting that he send questions as soon as he had them. During each update, I would provide detailed feedback and request that he ask questions. The questions never came. This caused issues because my comments were never directly addressed and/or answered. I was happy with the screens that were being provided, but after two months of patience and pulling teeth for this wireframe to be completed, I still could not confirm whether all the necessary screens had been included. A typical wireframe or flowchart shows clearly how each screen connects with the others and how the application will *flow*, yet I was never provided with that transparency. Only after multiple complaints did they finally use a wireframing application that allowed me to see each screen in clickable form. This assured me that any app created from this skeleton would work in the way I imagined. But we had yet to touch upon the functionality component of the app: another red flag. When the developer assigned my project to a design specialist, I learned that none of these individuals had ever worked with each other before. I was deeply concerned, as there were no clear instructions in the wireframe to confidently hand the project to someone who hadn't seen it evolve from scratch. The project manager, ideally in charge of ensuring clear communication between all parties, was MIA. It fell upon me to assume his role. This led to further delays of approval as I helped navigate the handoff in the hope that it wouldn't be a complete disaster. The owner also noticed the lags we were facing and quickly onboarded a programmer so we could begin discussing how the platform would actually be built.

At last, I had to accept the fact that I'd made a poor decision to work with this company. As time wore on, it became clear to me that the company owner was simply hiring individuals on the fly to meet project needs, without fully considering whether they could collaborate well together or how knowledge transfers would be handled. While explaining to the programmer my vision for the platform and explaining the wireframes, he revealed that he had no idea how to build what I wanted. The owner, who was on the call during this conversation, quickly realized his mistake. We went through two more programmers before I hit my boiling point. I let him know that I felt misled from the beginning. I requested a full refund and nullification of our contract, but the owner started pointing fingers at me, claiming to have lost more than the $9,000 that I'd already paid. He then requested the second payment before we continued any further. With no positive end in sight, I made one of the hardest financial decisions of my short business journey to date when I terminated the project and took the $9,000 loss, never to hear from them again. I considered suing the company for deception and for not providing services commensurate with what I'd paid, but the hassle and additional monetary losses didn't seem worth it.

At this point in my Drill Factory journey, I was relieved at not having to risk my entire savings, but I'd lost more than $9,000 in the form of motivation and self-confidence. Even with all the struggles I was dealing with, having to provide feedback and updates to the development company kept me pushing and actioning on key pieces of the project. Once that stopped, however, I was unsure of where to go next. I took some time away from things to set my thoughts straight. The pain of coming so close to achieving my goal and being deceived took its mental toll on me, and I found myself in a depressive state. I pushed my big idea aside and resorted to partying as a way to cope. My armor wasn't yet thick enough to deal with this kind of adversity.

After two months of pouting, I got out of my funk and into my vision. Knowing what I did wrong helped me see what was missing. I was happy that I was able to cut my losses and accept initial defeat. More importantly, I learned that in order to climb to the top, one had to stumble down into the valley. I threw myself into more networking events, opening my mind to the many possible opportunities and directions I might take. One connection, in particular, led me to an accelerator program based out of Massachusetts. The application involved submitting a business plan a $500 application fee, but a networking connection allowed me to waive that fee. Still, I didn't have a fully written plan on hand and had to create one on the fly. In the end, the judges decided not to accept me into the program, citing a lack of originality and cost analysis in an already competitive space. The feedback was a bummer to hear, but I welcomed it as an opportunity to craft a better product that would set me apart from the competition. Deep down, I knew they wouldn't accept me, but at least I had obtained constructive criticism at no cost. Now it was time to implement and make it happen.

I continued to attend networking events and obtain feedback on my newly updated business plan. Many people liked the idea and wanted to help any way they could, but I started to see a trend in their responses. "What's your proof of concept?" they would ask. "How do you know it will work?" I finally caved in, pivoting away from the animated functionality of a mobile app into a website of self-created training videos. To make this happen, I spent four days a week for five months, creating football-specific workouts. I hadn't trained so hard since college, so the strain on my body was grueling. Some weekends I couldn't do anything but rest. About three months into the content creation phase, I hired a video editor to tackle the mundane task of adding voice instructions that synced up with my movements. I found the video editor through a task provider and was able to negotiate the full editing of four hundred 30-second videos for a total of $5,000. $5,000 was a large sum of money, for sure, but a worthwhile investment in terms of quality and for its marketing potential across social media platforms. Being frugal in the world of business can backfire as we've learned from above. Things were moving in the right direction. The next step was to get my content ready for the web…and for the world.

Chapter 12: Creating a Business Plan

After taking the $9,000 loss, I was very cautious going forward. I stayed the e-commerce course, but more strategically than ever. Blank slate at the ready, I set off to create a detailed business plan. As luck would have it, I was speaking about my business goals to my gym partner, and he mentioned an accelerator program he was in called TLE Center for Urban Entrepreneurship (TLECFUE). TLECFUE is a non-profit urban development organization assisting with business development in underrepresented communities. The program educates individuals in everything one needs to be successful—including business taxes, credit, legal matters, presenting/pitching, and creating an overall business plan—and connects them with people who can help with this process. You're also assigned a mentor to assist in your growth outside the formal sessions.

By the end of the program, participants are given an opportunity to pitch their business ideas to a panel of investors for a chance at funding their dreams. Excited by the progress my gym partner made in his own journey, I asked if there was any way I could join, despite them being five weeks in. He was skeptical, but I wasn't going to stop asking unless rejected outright. He introduced me to the program's creator, Tricia Young, and she had me fill out a brief survey prior to acceptance. Fortunately, I'd seen these questions a year before when going after the previous accelerator program. Impressed by my efforts, she allowed me in. I was ecstatic! Not only did I have a plan of action, but now I also had the company of other driven individuals to lean on during the vulnerable times. Moreover, the group was there to hold me accountable for finishing what I started. Tricia, a business owner and consultant herself, was the business mentor I always needed.

Creating a Business Plan

While creating my business plan for The Drill Factory, the following steps were impressed upon me.

Describe the problem: Have you ever struggled with something in life and thought to yourself, "This would be so much easier if…"? This is how many businesses get started. We see a problem in our everyday lives and decide to do something about it. I started The Drill Factory in response to a need for a centralized athletic development platform, but I also needed to continue validating the problem to ensure it wasn't simply a personal one. Effective ways to gauge a wider need include online surveys, focus groups, and in-person interviews. This information becomes critical in the establishment of a viable business plan.

Describe the business/value proposition: Now that you've identified a problem that needs to be addressed, it's time to bring the business to life. This is where we make things overly complicated because we tend to push our ideas on the market rather than let the market decide what our business will be. It's important to have a grand idea of the business while establishing your "proof of concept." Typically, proof of concept is a low-cost version of your business or service that helps you gain insight as to the direction of your business. In this case, I took advantage of YouTube, providing workout packages to athletes for free to test their effectiveness. I asked them to send me videos of themselves performing the workouts to help me gauge their ability to mimic the videos without in-person instruction. You may wish to continue developing your proof of concept until it hits monetization to better make your case to investors in the event you're given an opportunity to pitch it. I believe strongly in providing value and services for free until customer loyalty is so strong that, out of sheer trust, they'll pay for anything you produce.

Describe the target market: In the case of The Drill Factory, I identified athletes, parents of athletes, and coaches as my target market. Athletes would be the ones using the platform for personal training and development. Parents would be advocates for their children, as well as primary contributors to making payments. The coaches would utilize the training material to develop their athletes beyond the playing season. Whatever your target market may be, it must be focused on specific segments over full populations. The more specific you can be about your target market, the better. Along with understanding your target market, you'll want to understand the industry it resides in. Is the industry as a whole profitable? Do any existing trends prove a need for what you're offering? Are there any barriers to entry (e.g. cost, laws and regulations, etc.)? Investors need to know your target industry has real growth potential. Even in today's retro culture, for example, you can be sure no one would ever invest in an internet company trying to bring back dial-up modems!

Competition: We want to believe we're the first and/or best ever to do whatever it is we do. This is rarely the case. We must understand our competitors' strengths and weaknesses better than we know our own. When interviewing or surveying your potential user base, don't be afraid to ask what they think about your competitors' offerings. Their likes, dislikes, and suggestions for improvement can be a goldmine for your business. Not only must you understand your biggest competitor(s) from a product/service improvement standpoint; you must also understand whether your differentiated business model can be successful in the market at all. Does your competitor have established brand loyalty? Do they already dominate the market? What is your strategy to take their customers? Or are there so many that competition isn't a factor? These are all things that should be considered and documented.

Strategic plan: So you've done all your homework and laid it all out on paper. Now's the time to plan your implementation and timing. Create a plan that addresses customer growth and product/service enhancement. Make sure you have an exit strategy in place for when you've hit a certain objective or financial landmark. This would give investors assurance that there's a light at the end of the tunnel for their investment dollars. Completely liquidating your position in a company isn't a requirement for an investor, but understanding what your long-term goal is would be helpful. For The Drill Factory, my strategy was to offer three to six months of free in-person training to local athletes to build awareness of my brand. Meanwhile, my website was being developed and I had three months allocated for focus groups and platform adjustments. Around nine months into the first year, I looked to increase awareness from a personal trainers' perspective for loading additional content onto the platform. After about eighteen months, I would start thinking more seriously about a mobile app as a means of growing my customer base.

Financial model: This is your chance to tabulate every foreseeable cost, projected revenue, and the financial statement associated with your business. The research you've done on your competitors' costs and revenues should be taken into account toward providing a realistic forecast of your own. Keep in mind, however, that even the soundest financial model is no more than an estimate based on projected results and will never fully reflect how the business will perform financially. If your business has been operating and you can provide actual cost/revenue numbers, then you'll be able to come up with a more realistic, attainable forecast.

Costs

Startup costs: These include any and every item required to be paid to get your business up and running. My initial startup costs were pretty straightforward: website development, logo design, and video content editing, to name a few. Because I drew from my own capital, I was able to leave out the financing fees normally associated with such costs. These items are your company's assets. They're typically presented on your balance sheet and depreciate in accordance with their asset life. Some costs are expensed in the same year, depending on value and expected use. Your accountant should be able to help you with these nuances.

Cost of goods sold: Cost of goods sold, or COGS, refers to the actual cost required to sell a product or service. Since The Drill Factory is a service business, my cost revolves around paying individual contractors or content providers for the revenue they generate on the website.

Operating cost: This is the cost associated with keeping your business running on a monthly basis. The Drill Factory is a website, so website hosting fees, monthly cloud server fees, and utilities, such as phone and electric, are all included. Without these, the website would cease to be.

Salaries: The point of a business isn't just to satisfy the needs of your customers, but also your need for an income. Leave room to pay yourself.

Revenue

And now, for the moment we've all been waiting for: revenue. At this point, it's best to layout your cash flow in terms of what you're offering before determining how much you'll charge for each product or service. The amount you charge will be based on research but also what you require to become profitable. Then you'll need to layout the number of monthly sales you project to generate over the next one to three years. This will help determine your gross profit—i.e., gross revenue less COGS. I listed out two product offerings: one subscription-based, the other an as-needed service. I used my competitors' pricing and offerings to determine an appropriate starting point for myself. Since *none* of my researched competitors were providing an amount of content compared to mine, I nudged my price point upward. Neither could any of my competitors boast of offering an as-needed service for online constructive criticism, so I calculated an estimated cost based on the survey results I'd collected while creating the platform. Note that your strategic plan must align with such revenue projections.

Financial statements: Financial statements combine and summarize all the information you've compiled before. They help investors track the health and long-term projections of your business. Financial statements include an income statement, which provides a snapshot of your profitability over the course of the year. The income statement accounts for profit, expenses, interest, depreciation, and taxes. Investors care deeply about these numbers. Most people know about net income (i.e., total revenue less total expenses), but investors will also want to understand your earnings before interest, tax, depreciation and amortization (EBITDA) and gross profit margin. The latter is calculated by subtracting the COGS from total revenue and dividing that number by total revenue. My three-year income statement presented a net loss until breaking even in year three. I was able to clearly show revenue growth and steady change in the bottom income line, which is all one can hope for in a startup company.

Balance sheet: The balance sheet reflects your business assets, liabilities, and stockholder equity at a point in time. Note the difference between a point in time for the balance sheet and the activity incurred over the course of a year for the income statement. Assets are items of value the company owns and utilize to keep the business operating and generating revenue. Liabilities are your company's financial obligations to be paid back on an agreed-upon date. Liabilities are associated with the purchase of assets or economic benefit. At this point, I had no financial obligations/liabilities that weren't prepaid. At some point, I'll need to pay my website content providers, which will result in certain monthly liabilities. The equity section displays your company's ownership spread, listing the value split between investors and any earnings kept within the company (retained earnings). The net income (loss) gets rolled into the retained earnings every year. As of writing this book, I'm the sole owner of The Drill Factory and would include nothing but retained earnings here. As the term "balance sheet" suggests, these financials must balance in order to be considered complete. Remember the balance sheet formula: Assets = Liabilities + Equity. If you've utilized a spreadsheet that pulls your financial data appropriately, the balance sheet should balance. Better yet, leave this step to your faithful accountant.

Cash flow statement: The cash flow statement shows how changes in your balance sheet and income statement accounts affect cash within the company. These changes are broken down into three buckets: operating, investing, and financing activities. The **operating** bucket includes cash inflow/outflow over the normal course of business. Investors like to look at operating cash flow, as it helps them truly understand a company's profitability by showing whether cash is effectively flowing into the business from operations (and not out of it). Examples of operating activities include accounts receivable, accounts payable, and purchasing and selling of inventory. The **investing** bucket details the cash inflow/outflow from investment gains/losses. This includes the purchase of a website or the selling of a fixed asset within the business. If the investing activities section of your cash flow statement is negative, it doesn't necessarily mean your company isn't robust. Your company could just as well be going through a heavy investment period to grow and scale the business, which requires a capital risk. The **financing** bucket involves cash movement between owners, debtors, and/or investors. Examples include obtaining capital through acquisition of a new debt instrument, reducing capital by paying off debt, issuing stock to increase capital, and more. Investors look to this section to see if the company has a sufficient line of capital and whether it's being managed appropriately. A healthy financing section shows a company's financial resilience against hardships.

The number of factors that might go into a financial statement can be overwhelming. If accounting isn't your strong suit, be prepared to bring a finance expert onboard or hire one temporarily to make yourself aware of how your business is functioning beyond day-to-day operations.

Results of the Program

Going into the program, I was expecting accountability from its structure and a space in which to focus on my goals. By the end of the program, I found myself at the receiving end of so much more. Until then, I hadn't even considered investors as a necessity, thinking I could fund the project myself. This became clearest to me during my two presentations, through which I was able to generate genuine interest in my project. After the first presentation, a woman introduced me to an economic development program that provides free services to businesses established in the city of Boston. I connected with the program manager and was able to get my $10,000+ website designed and built within two months at no cost. The second presentation didn't lead to an investment, but it did allow me to make connections with potential coaches for my platform, as well as with community centers for additional training and client opportunities. The takeaway from all of this? Do your research and document the process. The more information you have written down, the more realistic the business becomes.

Chapter 13: The Fruits of My Labor

It has been said when one door closes, another opens. So it is with this book, which tells me where I'm going by showing me where I've been. A periodic backward glance is sometimes all it takes to help us pivot in the right direction. Most of the time we don't believe we've done enough when in reality the trials and tribulations of life have taught us more than we can articulate. Future value rests not in success itself, but in the path to getting there.

Reflection

By implementing the strategies described in these pages between 2012 and 2019, I developed in leaps and bounds. Financially, I grew my net worth from negative $50,000, inclusive of car/student loan debt, to over $150,000 of investments and capital, with zero debt. I went from working odd summer jobs at $10 an hour to my first career job, bringing in a salary of $43,000 before eventually making over $90,000 a year. I'm able to save over 75% of my monthly paycheck by minimizing expenses, budgeting, and maximizing revenue. Not only am I capitalizing on opportunities I see in the workplace and online, but friends and family also come to me with investment opportunities to generate passive income.

I often wondered whether this journey to financial freedom was for me. Early on in the process, people chided me for being miserly or not "living enough." They tried to make me feel bad for not spending my money on random activities or material pleasures. I began asking myself whether they were right. Looking back at those moments of doubt, I'm thankful I stuck to my guns because even though I'm now freer than ever to afford such things, I have zero desire for them because my values have changed. I value time spent with family and friends. I value being able to grow a foundation for generations to come. The things that matter are now the things that inspire me. In addition to my excitement over long-term growth, I'm deeply aware of how various events impact my daily life. Whether it's the latest financial crash or emergence of a new company, I'm better able to assess the implications and potential risk of every opportunity with lucidity.

None of this has come about by luck, coincidence, or generational wealth, but through faith, consistency, and understanding of goals.

How I Did It

Focusing on Action

One of my biggest pet peeves when it comes to accomplishing goals is when my peers (and myself at times) get stuck in the idea phase but still feel like they're progressing by virtue of discussion. I love a good discussion on innovative ways to do better in life but love the action plan and implementation phase even more. Let's say a friend comes to me with a surefire way to make a quick buck. Letting excitement get the better of me, I schedule some time to discuss the risks and rewards associated with the venture in question. Once the risks start outweighing the rewards, I don my most optimistic hat to focus on what we might accomplish. After that, I take some time to understand the level of effort required to make it happen. Depending on my own situation, I may take immediate action or hold off on it for a later date. Having the extra time provides clarity and allows me to make an opportunity to work in my favor when I'm best prepared to capitalize on it.

Limiting Excuses

If I had a dollar for every time a friend told me they regretted not acting faster on an idea, I probably wouldn't have needed to write this book of financial advice in the first place. By focusing on action, however, I've learned to actually *make* things happen instead of merely *thinking* about how to make them happen. In my stretches of focusing on action, putting in hundred-hour work weeks wasn't unrealistic to me. This didn't mean I was limiting myself (I believe balance is important), but if scheduling what needed to happen meant missing out on other potentially important activities (like getting eight full hours of sleep), then I was prepared to take the hit. Ignoring my friends' invites to hang out, I looked at Monday through Sunday the same way: as an opportunity to progress and move forward. The concept of a "weekend" meant nothing to me. Now, however, I look at things a bit differently. A friend of mine who's been instrumental throughout this journey once put it this way: "I no longer say I'm too busy; only that it's not a priority at the moment." Focusing on priority makes me fully accountable for my decision. Saying I'm "too busy" is little more than an excuse, whereas "not a priority" is tougher to swallow and reminds me that I'm *consciously* not setting aside time for whatever the task may be. Working out, making an effort to see certain people, not scaling my business: there's accountability in all of these decisions, and taking charge of them is something for which all of much must strive. I, therefore, look at my net worth not as a badge of honor, but as a reminder of the labor I put into attaining financial freedom. Though I doubted myself at many points along the way, I found comfort in the process of moving forward, slowly but surely.

Patience

My biggest struggle by far was staying the course without rushing. We all like the idea of "getting rich quick." Join today and learn how to make a million dollars tomorrow? Sign me up! But ask anyone who epitomizes success how they got to where they are, and they're sure to tell you: not without patience. The trick for me was to find progressive ways to occupy my time, as my impatience was always at its highest during slow periods when not actioning or having the greatest day at work. I used my frustrations as fuel to say, "I need to make this happen ASAP," before exhausting myself beyond repair.

Next Steps

I believe my capital gains will start to grow more quickly now that I have viable systems in place, all the while helping others grow along with me.

I'll continue to purchase properties to fix and flip, increase my contributions to the stock market, build the ultimate sports training platform, and teach the next generation how to be a better version of me (albeit 15 years sooner). In fact, my ultimate goal is to retire from the 9-5 circuit and have enough investments to mentor youth in athletics, finances, and life on a grand scale.

In Closing

This journey started as a way to show my community various strategies for navigating through life. We all know capital drives development, and I like to use it for that very purpose. The more capital individual communities can generate through legitimate methods, the better we all become.

Let my gratitude be the seed investment to your own successful future.

Made in the USA
Lexington, KY
20 December 2019